POPE FRANCIS

The Works of Mercy

Pope Francis

THE WORKS OF MERCY

ORBIS BOOKS
Maryknoll, New York 10545

 **ORBIS BOOKS**
Maryknoll, New York 10545

 **Fathers and Brothers MARYKNOLL**™

Founded in 1970, Orbis Books endeavors to publish works that enlighten the mind, nourish the spirit, and challenge the conscience. The publishing arm of the Maryknoll Fathers and Brothers, Orbis seeks to explore the global dimensions of the Christian faith and mission, to invite dialogue with diverse cultures and religious traditions, and to serve the cause of reconciliation and peace. The books published reflect the views of their authors and do not represent the official position of the Maryknoll Society. To learn more about Maryknoll and Orbis Books, please visit our website at www.maryknollsociety.org.

English language edition, copyright © 2017 by Orbis Books, Box 302, Maryknoll, NY 10545-0302.

Originally published in Italian as *Le Opere di Misericordia*. Copyright © 2016 by Libreria Editrice Vaticana, 00120 Città del Vaticano. Selection of texts by Giuseppe Merola.

Manufactured in the United States of America

Library of Congress Cataloging-in-Publication Data

Names: Francis, Pope, 1936– author.
Title: The works of mercy / Pope Francis.
Other titles: Opere di misericordia. English
Description: English language edition. | Maryknoll : Orbis Books, 2017.
Identifiers: LCCN 2017002612 | ISBN 9781626982369 (pbk.)
Subjects: LCSH: Mercy. | Catholic Church—Doctrines.
Classification: LCC BV4647.M4 F7313 2017 | DDC 248.4/6—dc23
LC record available at https://lccn.loc.gov/2017002612

Contents

Foreword by James F. Keenan, SJ   vii

PART I

The Works of Mercy

Reflecting on the Works of Mercy   3

PART II

The Corporal Works of Mercy

Feeding the Hungry   31

Giving Drink to the Thirsty   44

Clothing the Naked   47

Welcoming the Stranger   54

Visiting the Sick   81

Visiting the Prisoner   90

Burying the Dead   107

CONTENTS

PART III

The Spiritual Works of Mercy

Counseling the Doubtful 113

Instructing the Ignorant 121

Admonishing Sinners 132

Consoling the Afflicted 139

Pardoning Offenses 149

Bearing Wrongs Patiently 164

Praying to God for the Living and the Dead 169

PART IV

Conclusion

Blessed Are the Merciful 187

Foreword

"One cannot understand a true Christian who is not merciful, just as one cannot comprehend God without his mercy. This is the epitomizing word of the Gospel: mercy. It is the fundamental feature of the face of Christ."

These words from Pope Francis, originally spoken during an Angelus delivered in the first week of his Jubilee Year of Mercy, reveal the trademark of this papacy, mercy. These same words appear twice on these pages: first, as Francis introduces us to the corporal works of mercy and, then, as he considers the spiritual works of mercy, reminding us that "in our life everything is a gift, it is all mercy." They are central to his thought, his life, his ministry, and they are the key to these pages, as well.

God is mercy, God treats us mercifully, by that mercy we become empowered to practice mercy, and by receiving mercy we can and must, then, go and do likewise.

Receiving Mercy

Since the beginning of his papacy, in one uncanny admission after another, Pope Francis told us that he had sinned and that later he experienced being forgiven. He needed, encountered, and received Christ's mercy. The merciful forgiveness that he received was hardly incidental to his life. All indications, all biographies, and all autobiographical comments highlight the tangible significance that Francis's encounter with mercy had on him. By it he was transformed; by it, he became free. Justified by God, he was freed of his sins and freed of any need to explain or justify himself. In his freedom, Francis became our own unapologetic pope, fearless in promoting the message of mercy.

Like Peter, who in his own sinfulness was confronted by the risen Christ, Francis encountered Christ at some point in his life and was touched by his mercy. Thus, he became a person capable of practicing that mercy. As he reminds us time and again, until we receive mercy, we do not have the grace to practice it. If we do not believe we need mercy, we cannot share it. If we have not received it, we cannot give it. We need the gift, so as to give it.

You can hear in these pages how he accompanies us with the message of mercy, a message that deeply touched him, before he ever summoned us. His own experience and the experience of every convicted Catholic shaped the Jubilee Year of Mercy, from its conception to its closing. The summons of the Jubilee Year was that double invitation: receive the gift and give it. It is the Gospel in miniature, reiterated by Francis.

In *Misericordiae Vultus*, the bull that launched the Jubilee Year, Pope Francis noted the centrality of mercy: "Jesus Christ is the face of the Father's mercy. These words

---

1. Pope Francis, *Misericordiae vultus: Bull of Indiction of the Extraordinary Jubilee Year of Mercy* (April 11, 2015) para. 1. w2.vatican.va/

might well sum up the mystery of the Christian faith."[1] Later that year, a book-length interview with him was entitled *The Name of God is Mercy*. It highlighted the scandalous pervasiveness and inclusiveness of God's mercy. As the pope insisted, God "does not want anyone to be lost. His mercy is infinitely greater than our sins, his medicine is infinitely stronger than our illnesses that he has to heal." Without that mercy, we do not really know the Lord. "Only he who has been touched and caressed by the tenderness of his mercy really knows the Lord."[2] Here we hear the pope's own experiential familiarity with healing mercy, knowing its balm and inviting us to embrace it. Receiving mercy, we are then sent to be merciful.

When he announced the upcoming Jubilee Year, Pope Francis proclaimed that the mercy of God "excludes no one."[3] This inclusive claim was demonstrated, among other ways, by his extension to all priests the right to absolve anyone who procured an abortion.[4] In a similar way, Cardinal Oswald Gracias of Mumbai, one of Pope Francis's Group of Nine, spoke out against an Indian law that sought to criminalize being gay, becoming India's first religious leader to take such a stance, precisely on the opening day of the Jubilee Year. *New Ways Ministry* publicized the interview

content/francesco/en/bulls/documents/papa-francesco_bolla_20150411_misericordiae-vultus.html.

2. Pope Francis, *The Name of God is Mercy* (New York: Random House, 2016), 334.

3. Pope Francis, "Letter," September 1, 2015. https://w2.vatican.va/content/francesco/en/letters/2015/documents/papa-francesco_20150901_lettera-indulgenza-giubileo-misericordia.html.

4. Ibid.

with the banner, "As Year of Mercy Begins, Cardinal Says Being Gay is Not a Crime."[5] It is hard to think of any two topics that our bishops have more critiqued than abortion and homosexuality, but now, without any concern for scandal, the pope and the cardinal help us to see that the mercy of God is prior to all gospel messages.

Throughout the Jubilee Year, in many other ways, Pope Francis encouraged us to approach the altar of mercy with confidence and hope.

Practicing Mercy

Now with this book Pope Francis instructs us again, though this time he emphasizes less the summons to receive mercy and more the command to practice it. As he accompanied us to encounter mercy, he now stands with us as he teaches us to live mercy. Of course, he never misses the opportunity to remind us that mercy is always available for every person, that the possibility of redemption is always at hand. As he instructs us in the spiritual work of counseling the doubtful, "Even if the life of a person has been a disaster, even if it is destroyed by vices, drugs, or anything else— God is in this person's life."

Still, for the most part, he is training us to be merciful. Having been healed by mercy, we can become imitators of the God in whose image we are made. And so, in answer to Christ's call to follow him, we practice mercy.

---

5. Robert Shine, "As Year of Mercy Begins, Cardinal Says Being Gay is Not a Crime," *New Ways Ministry Blog,* December 8, 2015, https://newwaysministryblog.wordpress.com/2015/12/08/as-year-of-mercy-begins-cardinal-says-being-gay-is-not-a-crime/.

Make no mistake about it: Mercy is not one virtue and set of practices among others. Mercy is the "epitomizing word of the Gospel." Here the scriptures are unambiguous: mercy is the *condition* for salvation. This is made clear in the parable about the last judgment (in Matthew 25), where salvation is offered simply for those who have performed what were later called the corporal works of mercy. Like the story of the rich man who never sees poor Lazarus at his gate, we will be judged by our practice of mercy (Lk 16: 19–31).

Mercy is at the heart of our theological tradition. One could argue that our entire theological tradition is expressed in terms of mercy, which I define as the willingness to enter into the chaos of another.[6] Understood in such terms, creation itself is an act of mercy that brings order into the chaos of the universe. The incarnation is God's entry into the chaos of human existence. And the redemption is bringing us out of the chaos of our slavery to sin. Because God is merciful, every action of God is aimed at entering our chaos.

The defining acts of God are merciful, and the same can be said of the acts of the early Church. Christianity defined itself precisely in terms of mercy. In his wonderful work *The Rise of Christianity*, Rodney Stark argues that "Christianity was an urban movement, and the New Testament was set down by urbanites." But those urban areas were dreadful. Stark describes the conditions as "social chaos and chronic urban misery."[7]

---

6. James F. Keenan, *The Works of Mercy: The Heart of Catholicism* (Lanham: Rowman and Littlefield, 2005).

7. Rodney Stark, *The Rise of Christianity* (Princeton: Princeton University Press, 1996), 147.

Greco-Roman cities were not settled places. Given high infant mortality and short life expectancy, these cities required a steady and substantial influx of newcomers simply to maintain population levels. As a result, the cities were comprised of immigrant strangers.

Moreover, Christianity was distinctive in its response to these new arrivals. While the gods of the pagan religions imposed ethical obligations, these were substantively ritualistic, not neighbor directed. In fact, Roman culture did not promote mercy or pity. Since mercy implied "unearned help or relief," it was considered contradictory to justice. For Roman philosophers, mercy was "a defect of character unworthy of the wise and excusable only in those who had not yet grown up. It was an impulsive response based on ignorance." Stark concludes: "This was the moral climate in which Christianity taught that mercy is one of the primary virtues—that a merciful God requires humans to be merciful. Moreover, the corollary that *because* God loves humanity, Christians may not please God unless they *love one another* was entirely new." He adds: "Perhaps even more revolutionary was the principle that Christian love and charity must extend beyond the boundaries of family and tribe, that it must extend to 'all those who in every place call on the name of our Lord Jesus Christ' (1 Cor 1:2)."[8]

The Works of Mercy

The practice of mercy must always be specific, and so in these pages Francis descends into the particularity of each of the seven corporal and each of the seven spiritual works

---

8. Ibid., 212.

of mercy. He leads us into each of the works to see how capacious they are. Summoning us, for instance, to visit the prisoner, he leads us to reflect on the condition of prisoners, on their marginality and isolation, on their need for hope. He speaks of his own visits to prisoners, of seeing tears of hope in the faces of those who encounter a welcoming visitor, of entering into solidarity with the plight of prisoners, realizing that just as prisoners must reform, so too must the society that builds prisons. Inviting us to see prisoners and the effects of imprisonment, he invites us to consider that the work is to accompany the person not only within the prison but also when that person is released and re-entering society, looking to find a way of reintegration.

Where does he get these fourteen works of mercy from?

The first six of the corporal works of mercy (feed the hungry, give drink to the thirsty, shelter the homeless, clothe the naked, visit the sick, and visit the imprisoned) were derived from the parable of the last judgment in Matthew 25:34–45. It took some time to name a seventh, "bury the dead," but with this addition the corporal works could parallel perfectly other groups of seven, such as the seven sacraments, the seven deadly sins, and the virtues (four cardinal; three theological).

The spiritual works were developed in both Eastern and Western Christianity during patristic times. In the early literature, the original corporal works often had spiritual counterparts: the spiritually hungry, naked, thirsty, and so on. Origen recognized that Matthew 25 was not only a call to dress the body with clothes or to feed it with food but also a summons to tend to the spiritual needs of the other. In many ways the roots of the call came through the appreciation of the Christian as being one—body and soul. Preachers from Origen through John Chrysostom warned listeners to attend not only to their neighbors' physical nourishment but also to their need for the word of God.

Such concerns were often accompanied by another set of issues. The epistles urged Christians to pardon, to give mutual support, and to exhort each other (as in Ephesians 4:32 and Colossians 3:13, 16). These biblical recommendations too were looking for a home in the emerging tradition of the Church. Indeed, in 2 Corinthians 5, Paul urges his readers to become ambassadors of reconciliation, imitating the very action of God in reconciling the world. If the Christian is the follower of Christ the Incarnate One, then the Christian is called to do what Christ did: reconcile.

This call to reconciliation, along with the call to be vigilant about the spiritual needs of the other, eventually coalesced into the six spiritual works of mercy. When Augustine wrote the *Enchiridioni* in 421, he proposed the corporal works of mercy and added three spiritual ones: to console the afflicted, to show the way to the lost, to assist those who hesitate. This threesome was an invitation to be vigilant for one's neighbor's spiritual needs. After proposing these three, Augustine offered a second set, revolving around pardon. As he wrote, pardoning is not only a matter of forgiving sins and bearing wrongs; it also includes correcting and rebuking the sinner; this too is mercy.

Augustine then turned to the last work, praying for the living and the dead. On first glance, this seventh work seemed an easy parallel to the seventh corporal work, but for Augustine, praying for the living and the dead was a prayer that extended even to one's enemies. The prayer for the living and the dead was then the summary work of the first six spiritual practices. For this list, the seventh brought the Christian into a spiritual fellowship with all Christians.

Read in these pages then about the sinner whose encounter with God's mercy freed him for a life of mercy that excludes no one and for a way of accompanying us scandalously so that we may learn to go and do likewise.

James F. Keenan, SJ
Canisius Professor
Boston College

I
THE WORKS OF MERCY

Reflecting on
the Works of Mercy

In this Holy Year, we look forward to the experience of opening our hearts to those living on the outermost fringes of society, fringes that modern society itself creates. How many uncertain and painful situations there are in the world today! How many are the wounds borne by the flesh of those who have no voice because their cry is muffled and drowned out by the indifference of the rich! During this Jubilee, the Church will be called even more to heal these wounds, to assuage them with the oil of consolation, to bind them with mercy and cure them with solidarity and vigilant care. Let us not fall into humiliating indifference or a monotonous routine that prevents us from discovering what is new! Let us ward off destructive cynicism! Let us open our eyes and see the misery of the world, the wounds of our brothers and sisters who are denied their dignity, and let us recognize that we are compelled to heed their cry for help! May we reach out to them and support them so they can feel the warmth of our presence, our friendship, and our fraternity! May their cry become our own, and together may we break down the barriers of indifference that too often reign supreme and mask our hypocrisy and egoism!

It is my burning desire that, during this Jubilee, the Christian people may reflect on the *corporal and spiritual works of mercy*. It will be a way to reawaken our conscience, too often grown dull in the face of poverty. And let us enter more deeply into the heart of the Gospel where the poor have a special experience of God's mercy. Jesus introduces us to these works of mercy in his preaching so that we can know whether or not we are living as his disciples. Let us rediscover the *corporal works of mercy*: to feed the hungry, give drink to the thirsty, clothe the naked, welcome the stranger, heal the sick, visit the imprisoned, and bury the dead. And let us not forget the *spiritual works of mercy*: to counsel the doubtful, instruct the ignorant, admonish sinners, comfort the afflicted, forgive offences, bear patiently those who do us ill, and pray for the living and the dead.

We cannot escape the Lord's words to us, and they will serve as the criteria upon which we will be judged: whether we have fed the hungry and given drink to the thirsty, welcomed the stranger and clothed the naked, or spent time with the sick and those in prison (cf. Mt 25:31–45). Moreover, we will be asked if we have helped others to escape the doubt that causes them to fall into despair and is often a source of loneliness; if we have helped to overcome the ignorance in which millions of people live, especially children deprived of the necessary means to free themselves from the bonds of poverty; if we have been close to the lonely and afflicted; if we have forgiven those who have offended us and have rejected all forms of anger and hate that lead to violence; if we have had the kind of patience shown by God, who is so patient with us; and if we have commended our brothers and sisters to the Lord in prayer. In each of these "little ones," Christ himself is present. His flesh becomes visible in the flesh of the tortured, the crushed, the scourged, the malnourished, and the exiled...to be acknowledged, touched, and cared for by us. Let us not forget the words of Saint John of the Cross: "As we prepare to leave this life, we will be judged on the basis of love" (*Words of Light and Love*, 57).

—Misericordiae Vultus, *15*

THE CONCRETENESS OF FAITH

We can make many pastoral plans, conceive of new methods for drawing people close, but if we don't take the path of God who has come in the flesh, of the Son of God who became man in order to walk with us, then we are not on the path of the good spirit. Instead what prevails is the antichrist, worldliness, the spirit of the world.

How many people do we find in life who seem spiritual but who do not speak of doing works of mercy? Why is this? Because the works of mercy are precisely the concrete sign of our confession that the Son of God has come in the flesh: visiting the sick, feeding those who do not have food, taking care of the outcast. We must perform works of mercy, therefore, because each of our brothers and sisters, whom we must love, is the flesh of Christ: God has come in the flesh to identify himself with us, and in those who who suffer it is Christ who suffers.

—*Morning Homilies, January 7, 2016*

A Field Hospital

I see clearly that the thing the Church needs most today is the ability to heal wounds and to warm the hearts of the faithful; it needs nearness, proximity. I see the Church as a field hospital after battle. It is useless to ask a seriously injured person if he has high cholesterol and about the level of his blood sugar! You have to heal his wounds. Then we can talk about everything else. Heal the wounds, heal the wounds... And you have to start from the ground up.

The Church sometimes has locked itself up in small things, in small-minded rules. The most important thing is the first proclamation: Jesus Christ has saved you. And the ministers of the Church must be ministers of mercy above all... In pastoral ministry we must accompany people, and we must heal their wounds.

— *"A Big Heart Open to God,"* Interview in America,
September 30, 2013

The Capacity for Mercy

God's mercy transforms human hearts; it enables us, through the experience of a faithful love, to become merciful in turn. In an ever-new miracle, divine mercy shines forth in our lives, inspiring each of us to love our neighbor and to devote ourselves to what the Church's tradition calls the spiritual and corporal works of mercy. These works remind us that faith finds expression in concrete, everyday actions meant to help our neighbors in body and spirit: by feeding, visiting, comforting, and instructing them. On such things will we be judged. For this reason, I expressed my hope that "the Christian people may reflect on the corporal and spiritual works of mercy; this will be a way to reawaken our conscience, too often grown dull in the face of poverty, and to enter more deeply into the heart of the Gospel where the poor have a special experience of God's mercy" (*Misericordiae Vultus*, 15). For in the poor, the flesh of Christ "becomes visible in the flesh of the tortured, the crushed, the scourged, the malnourished, and the exiled...to be acknowledged, touched, and cared for by us" (*ibid.*). It is the unprecedented and scandalous mystery of the extension in time of the suffering of the Innocent Lamb, the burning bush of gratuitous love. Before this love, we can, like Moses, take off our sandals (cf. Ex 3:5), especially when the poor are our brothers or sisters in Christ who are suffering for their faith.

In the light of this love, which is as strong as death (cf. Song 8:6), the real poor are revealed as those who refuse to see themselves as such. They consider themselves rich, but they are actually the poorest of the poor. This is because they are slaves to sin, which leads them to use wealth and power not for the service of God and others, but to stifle within their hearts the profound sense that they too are only poor beggars. The greater their power and wealth, the more this blindness and deception can grow. It can even reach the point of being blind to Lazarus begging at their doorstep (cf. Lk 16:20–21). Lazarus, the poor man, is a figure of Christ who through the poor pleads for our conversion. As such, he represents the possibility of conversion that God offers us and that we may well fail to see.

Such blindness is often accompanied by the proud illusion of our own omnipotence, which reflects in a sinister way the diabolical "you will be like God" (Gen 3:5), which is the root of all sin. This illusion can likewise take social and political forms, as shown by the totalitarian systems of the twentieth century, and, in our own day, by the ideologies of monopolizing thought and technoscience, which would make God irrelevant and reduce man to raw material to be exploited. This illusion can also be seen in the sinful structures linked to a model of false development based on the idolatry of money, which leads to lack of concern for the fate of the poor on the part of wealthier individuals and societies; they close their doors, refusing even to see the poor.

For all of us, then, the season of Lent in this Jubilee Year is a favorable time to overcome our existential alienation by listening to God's word and by practicing the works of mercy. In the corporal works of mercy we touch the flesh of Christ in our brothers and sisters who need to be fed, clothed, sheltered, visited; in the spiritual works of mercy—counsel, instruction, forgiveness, admonishment, and prayer—we touch more directly our own sinfulness. The corporal and spiritual works of mercy must never be separated. By touching the flesh of the crucified Jesus in those who are suffering, sinners can receive the gift of recognizing that they too are poor and in need. By taking this path, the "proud," the "powerful," and the "wealthy" spoken of in the *Magnificat* have the possibility of realizing that they are embraced and undeservedly loved by the crucified Lord who died and rose for them. This love alone is the answer to that yearning for infinite happiness and love that we think we can satisfy with the idols of knowledge, power, and riches. Yet the danger always remains that by a constant refusal to open the doors of their hearts to Christ who, in the form of the poor, knocks on those doors, the proud, the rich, and the powerful will end up condemning themselves and plunging into the eternal abyss of solitude which is Hell. The pointed words of Abraham apply to them and to all of us: "They have Moses and the prophets; let them hear them" (Lk 16:29). Such attentive listening will best prepare us to celebrate the final victory over sin and death of the Bridegroom, now risen, who desires to purify his Betrothed in expectation of his coming.

—*Message for Lent 2016, 3*

MARY OUR MOTHER

In the silence, we will hear what she says to us once more, "What, my most precious little one, saddens your heart?" (*Nican Mopohua*, 107). "Yet am I not here with you, I who have the honor of being your mother?" (*ibid.*, 119).

Mary tells us that she has "the honor" of being our mother, assuring us that the tears of those who suffer are not in vain. They are a silent prayer rising to heaven, always finding a place under Mary's mantle. In her and with her, God has made himself our brother and companion along the journey; he carries our crosses with us so as not to leave us overwhelmed by our sufferings.

"Am I not your mother? Am I not here? Do not let trials and pains overwhelm you," she tells us. Today, she sends us out anew, as she did Juancito. Today, she comes to tell us again: "Be my ambassador, the one I send to build many new shrines, accompany many lives, wipe away many tears. Simply be my ambassador by walking along the paths of your neighborhood, of your community, of your parish." We can build shrines by sharing the joy of knowing that we are not alone, that Mary accompanies us. "Be my ambassador," she says to us, "giving food to the hungry, drink to those who thirst, a refuge to those in need, clothing the naked and visiting the sick. Come to the aid of those in prison; do not leave them alone. Forgive whoever has offended you, console the grieving, be patient with others, and above all beseech and pray to our God."

"Am I not your mother? Am I not here with you?" Mary says this to us again. "Go and build my shrine, help me to lift up the lives of my sons and daughters who are your brothers and sisters."

—*Homily at the Basilica of Our Lady of Guadalupe,*
Mexico City, February 13, 2016

IN SOLIDARITY WITH THOSE WHO SUFFER

We know that Jesus wanted to show solidarity with every person. He wanted everyone to experience his companionship, his help, his love. He identified with all those who suffer, who weep, who suffer any kind of injustice. He tells us this clearly: "I was hungry and you gave me food, I was thirsty and you gave me something to drink; I was a stranger and you welcomed me" (Mt 25:35).

Faith makes us know that God is at our side, that God is in our midst and his presence spurs us to charity. Charity is born of the call of a God who continues to knock on our door, the doors of all people, to invite us to love, to compassion, to service of one another.

Jesus keeps knocking on our doors, the doors of our lives. He doesn't do this by magic, with special effects, with flashing lights and fireworks. Jesus keeps knocking on our door in the faces of our brothers and sisters, in the faces of our neighbors, in the faces of those by our side.

— Visit with the homeless at Saint Patrick's Parish,
Washington, DC, September 24, 2015

FORGIVE US LORD

Immigrants dying at sea, in boats that were vehicles of hope and became vehicles of death. That is how the headlines put it. Since first hearing of this tragedy a few weeks ago, a tragedy that has happened all too frequently, the memory of it has stayed with me like a painful thorn in my heart. So I felt that I had to come here today, to pray and to offer a sign of my closeness, but also to challenge our consciences lest this tragedy be repeated. Please, let it not be repeated!

First, however, I want to say a word of heartfelt gratitude and encouragement to you, the people of Lampedusa and Linosa, and to the various associations, volunteers, and security personnel who continue to attend to the needs of people journeying toward a better future. You are so few, and yet you offer an example of solidarity! Thank you! I also thank Archbishop Francesco Montenegro for all his help, his efforts, and his pastoral care. I offer a cordial greeting to Mayor Giusi Nicolini: Thank you so much for what you have done and are doing. I also think with affection of those Muslim immigrants who this evening begin the fast of Ramadan, which I trust will bear abundant spiritual fruit. The Church is at your side as you seek a more dignified life for yourselves and your families. To all of you: *o'scià!*

This morning, in the light of God's word which has just been proclaimed, I wish to offer some thoughts meant to challenge people's consciences and lead them to reflection and a concrete change of heart.

"Adam, where are you?" This is the first question which God asks man after his sin. "Adam, where are you?" Adam lost his bearings, his place in creation, because he thought he could be powerful, able to control everything; he thought he could be God. Harmony was lost; man erred and this error occurs over and over again in our relationships with others. "The other" is no longer a brother or a sister to be loved, but simply someone who disturbs my life and my comfort. God asks a second question: "Cain, where is your brother?" The illusion of being powerful, of being as great as God, even of being God himself, leads to a whole series of errors, a chain of death, even to the spilling of a brother's blood!

God's two questions echo even today, as forcefully as ever! How many of us, myself included, have lost our bearings? We are no longer attentive to the world in which we live; we don't care; we don't protect what God created for everyone, and we end up unable even to care for one another! And when humanity as a whole loses its bearings, the result is tragedy, such as the one we have just witnessed.

"Where is your brother? His blood cries out to me," says the Lord. This is not a question directed to others; it is a question directed to me, to you, to each of us. These brothers and sisters of ours were trying to escape difficult situations to find some serenity and peace. They were looking for a better place for themselves and their families, but instead they found death. How often do such people fail to find understanding, fail to find acceptance, fail to find solidarity? And their cry rises up to God! Once again I thank you, the people of Lampedusa, for your solidarity. I recently listened to one of these brothers of ours. Before arriving here, he and the others were at the mercy of traffickers, people who exploit the poverty of others, people who live off the misery of others. How much these people have suffered! Some of them never made it here.

"Where is your brother?" Who is responsible for this blood? In Spanish literature we have a comedy by Lope de Vega about the people of the town of Fuente Ovejuna killing their governor because he is a tyrant. They do it in such a way that no one knows who the actual killer is. So when the royal judge asks: "Who killed the governor?" they all reply: "Fuente Ovejuna, sir." Everybody and nobody! Today too, the question has to be asked: "Who is responsible for the blood of these brothers and sisters of ours?" "Nobody!" Every one of us has the same answer: "It isn't me; I don't have anything to do with it; it must be someone else, but certainly not me." Yet God is asking each of us: "Where is the blood of your brother that cries out to me?" Today no one in our world feels responsible. We have lost a sense of responsibility for our brothers and sisters. We have fallen into the hypocrisy of the priest and the Levite whom Jesus described in the parable of the Good Samaritan. We see our brother half dead on the side of the road and perhaps we say to ourselves, "Poor soul...!" and then we go on our way. It's not our responsibility, and with that we feel reassured, assuaged. The culture of comfort, which makes us think only of ourselves, makes us insensitive to the cries of other people, makes us live in soap bubbles which, however lovely, are insubstantial; they offer a fleeting and empty illusion that results in indifference to others. Indeed, it even leads to the globalization of indifference. In this globalized world, we have fallen into globalized indifference. We have become used to the suffering of others: "It doesn't affect me; it doesn't concern me; it's none of my business!"... The globalization of indifference has made us all anonymous, responsible, yet nameless and faceless.

"Adam, where are you? Where is your brother?" These are the two questions that God asks at the dawn of human history, that he asks each man and woman in our own day, and that he also asks us. But I would like us to ask a third question: "Who among us has wept because of this situation and others like it?" Has any one of us grieved for the death of these brothers and sisters? Has any one of us wept for these persons who were on the boat? For the young mothers carrying their babies? For the men who were looking for a way of supporting their families?

We are a society that has forgotten how to weep, how to experience compassion—"suffering with" others. The globalization of indifference has taken from us the ability to weep! In the Gospel we have heard the crying, the wailing, the great lamentation: "Rachel weeps for her children ...because they are no more." Herod sowed death to protect his own comfort, his own soap bubble. And so it continues

...Let us ask the Lord to remove the part of Herod that lurks in our hearts. Let us ask the Lord for the grace to weep over our indifference, to weep over the cruelty of our world, of our own hearts, and of all those who in anonymity make social and economic decisions that open the door to tragic situations like this. "Has anyone wept?" Today has anyone wept in our world?

Lord, in this liturgy, a penitential liturgy, we beg forgiveness for our indifference to so many of our brothers and sisters. Father, we ask your pardon for those who are complacent and closed amid comforts that have deadened their hearts. We beg your forgiveness for those who by their decisions on the global level have created situations that lead to these tragedies. Forgive us, Lord!

Today too, Lord, we hear you asking: "Adam, where are you? Where is the blood of your brother?"

—*Homily, visit to Lampedusa, July 8, 2013*

An Encounter of Love

To encounter Jesus is to experience his love. This love transforms us and makes us able to transmit to others the power it gives. In a way we could say that from the day of our baptism each one of us is given a new name in addition to the one given to us by our mom and dad; this name is "Christopher." We are all "Christophers." What does that mean? "Bearers of Christ." It is the name of our attitude, the attitude of a bearer of the joy of Christ, of the mercy of Christ. Every Christian is a "Christopher," that is, a bearer of Christ!

The mercy that we receive from the Father is not given as a private consolation, but makes us instruments so that others too might receive the same gift. There is a wonderful interplay between mercy and mission. Experiencing mercy renders us missionaries of mercy, and to be missionaries allows us to grow ever more in the mercy of God. Therefore, let us take our Christian calling seriously and commit to live as believers, because only then can the Gospel touch a person's heart and open it to receive the grace of love, to receive this great, all-welcoming mercy of God.

—Jubilee Audience, January 30, 2016

MEDIATOR OF MERCY

In this Year of Mercy we too can do the work of acting as mediators of mercy through the works of mercy in order to approach, to give relief, to create unity. So many good things can be done.

God's mercy always operates to save. It is quite the opposite of the work of those who always act to kill: for example, those who wage war. The Lord, through his servant Moses, guides Israel in the desert as if Israel were a son, educates the people to the faith, and makes a covenant with Israel, creating a bond of the strongest love, like that of a father with his child and of a groom with his bride.

Divine mercy goes that far. God offers a special, exclusive, privileged relationship of love. When he gives instructions to Moses regarding the covenant, he says: "If you will obey my voice and keep my covenant, you shall be my own possession among all peoples; for all the earth is mine, and you shall be to me a kingdom of priests and a holy nation" (Ex 19:5–6).

Of course, God already possesses all the earth because he created it; but his people become for him a different, special possession: his personal "reserve of gold and silver" such as King David stated he had given for the construction of the Temple.

So we become thus for God, by accepting his covenant and letting ourselves be saved by him. The Lord's mercy renders man precious, like a personal treasure that belongs to him, which he safeguards and with which he is well pleased.

These are the wonders of divine mercy, which reaches complete fulfillment in the Lord Jesus, in the "new and eternal covenant" consummated in his blood, which annuls our sin with forgiveness and renders us definitively children of God (cf. 1 Jn 3:1), precious gems in the hands of the good and merciful Father. And as we are children of God and have the opportunity to receive this legacy—that of goodness and mercy—in our relations with others, let us ask the Lord in this Year of Mercy that we too may do merciful things. Let us open our hearts in order to reach everyone with the works of mercy, to work the merciful inheritance bequeathed to us by God the Father.

—General Audience, Saint Peter's Square, January 27, 2016

BEING GOOD SAMARITANS

Today, here in Rome and in all the dioceses of the world, as we pass through the Holy Door, we also want to remember another door, a door that fifty years ago the Fathers of the Second Vatican Council opened to the world. This anniversary cannot be remembered only for the legacy of the Council's documents, which testify to a great advance in faith. Before all else, the Council was an encounter. A genuine *encounter between the Church and the men and women of our time.* An encounter marked by the power of the Spirit, who impelled the Church to emerge from the shoals which for years had kept her self-enclosed so as to set out once again, with enthusiasm, on her missionary journey. It was the resumption of a journey of encountering people where they live: in their cities and homes, in their workplaces. Wherever there are people, the Church is called to reach out to them and to bring the joy of the Gospel, and the mercy and forgiveness of God. Five decades later, we again take up this missionary drive with the same power and enthusiasm. The Jubilee challenges us to this openness, and demands that we not neglect *the spirit which emerged from Vatican II, the spirit of the Samaritan,* as Blessed Paul VI expressed it at the conclusion of the Council. May our passing through the Holy Door today commit us to making our own the mercy of the Good Samaritan.

—*Homily, Mass for the opening of the Holy Door for the Jubilee of Mercy, Saint Peter's Square, December 8, 2015*

A SOBER STYLE

Today, the Son of God is born, and everything changes. The Savior of the world comes to partake of our human nature; no longer are we alone and forsaken. The Virgin offers us her son as the beginning of a new life. The true light has come to illumine our lives so often beset by the darkness of sin. Today we once more discover who we are! Tonight we have been shown the way to reach the journey's end. Now must we put away all fear and dread, for the light shows us the path to Bethlehem. We must not be laggards; we are not permitted to stand idle. We must set out to see our Savior lying in a manger. This is the reason for our joy and gladness: this Child has been "born to us"; he was "given to us," as Isaiah proclaims (cf. 9:5). To a people who for two thousand years have traversed all the pathways of the world in order that every man and woman might share in this joy is now given the mission of making known the "Prince of peace" and becoming his effective servant in the midst of the nations.

So when we hear tell of the birth of Christ, let us be silent and let the Child speak. In rapt contemplation of his face let us engrave his words on our heart. If we take him in our arms and let ourselves be embraced by him, he will bring us unending peace of heart. This Child teaches us what is truly essential in our lives. He was born into the poverty of this world; there was no room at the inn for him and his family. He found shelter and support in a stable and was laid in a manger for animals. And yet, from this nothingness, the light of God's glory shines forth. From now on, the way of authentic liberation and perennial redemption is open to every man and woman who is simple of heart. This Child, whose face radiates the goodness, mercy, and love of God the Father, trains us, his disciples, as Saint Paul says, "to reject godless ways" and the richness of the world in order to live "temperately, justly and devoutly" (Ti 2:12).

In a society so often intoxicated by consumerism and hedonism, wealth and extravagance, appearances and narcissism, this Child calls us to act *soberly*, in other words, in a way that is simple, balanced, consistent, capable of seeing and doing what is essential. In a world that all too often is merciless to the sinner and lenient to the sin, we need to cultivate a strong sense of justice, to discern and to do God's will. Amid a culture of indifference that not infrequently turns ruthless, our style of life should instead be *devout*, filled with empathy, compassion, and mercy, drawn daily from the wellspring of prayer.

—*Homily, Midnight Mass, Nativity of the Lord, December 24, 2015*

MOVING FORWARD TOGETHER

Jesus is the path and *a path is for walking and following*. Now I want first of all to thank the Lord for your commitment to following him, and for your effort and suffering within the prison walls. Let us continue to trust him. He will give your heart hope and joy! I want to thank him for all of you who are generously dedicated to works of mercy here in Cagliari and in all of Sardinia. I would like to encourage you to continue on this path, to move forward together, striving to preserve among you first and foremost charity. This is very important.

We cannot follow Jesus on the path of love unless we first love others, unless we force ourselves to work together, to understand each other and to forgive each another, recognizing our own limitations and mistakes. We must do works of mercy—and with mercy! Putting our heart into them. Works of charity with love, with tenderness, and always with humility!

—Meeting with the poor and prisoners, Cathedral of Cagliari, Sardinia, September 22, 2013

To See Jesus in a Person Who Is in Need

In a world which, unfortunately, has been damaged by the virus of indifference, the works of mercy are the best antidote. In fact, they educate us to be attentive to the most basic needs of "the least of these my brethren" (Mt 25:40), in whom Jesus is present. Jesus is always present there. Where there is need, there is someone who has need, be it material or spiritual. Jesus is there. Recognizing his face in those who are in need is one way to really confront indifference. He allows us to be always vigilant, to avoid having Christ pass by without our recognizing him. It recalls to mind the words of St. Augustine: *"Timeo Iesum ranseuntem"* (Serm. 88, 14, 13): "I fear the Lord passing by," and I do not notice him; I fear that the Lord may pass before me in one of these little people in need, and I do not realize that it is Jesus. I fear that the Lord may pass by without my recognizing him! I wondered why St. Augustine said he *feared* the passing by of Jesus. The answer, unfortunately, is in our behavior: because we are often distracted, indifferent, and when the Lord comes close to approach us, we lose the opportunity to encounter him.

The works of mercy reawaken in us the need, and the ability, to make the faith alive and active with charity. I am convinced that, through these simple, daily actions, we can achieve a true cultural revolution, as happened in the past. If every one of us, every day, does one of these works, there would be a revolution in the world! Everyone, each and every one of us.

How many saints are remembered even today, not for the great works that they accomplished, but for the charity that they knew how to impart! We think of the recently canonized Mother Teresa. We do not remember her because of the many houses she opened around the world, but because she bent down to every person she found in the middle of the street in order to restore that person's dignity. How many abandoned children did she enfold in her arms; how many moribund people did she accompany to eternity, holding their hands! Such works of mercy are the features of the face of Jesus Christ, who takes care of his littlest brethren in order to bring the tenderness and closeness of God to each of them. May the Holy Spirit help us. May the Holy Spirit kindle within us the desire to live this way of life—at least once a day, at least! Let us again learn the corporal and spiritual works of mercy by heart, and ask the Lord to help us put them into practice every day, and at every moment when we see Jesus in a person who is in need.

—General Audience, Saint Peter's Square, October 12, 2016

A WAY OF LIFE

It is good to never forget that mercy is not an abstract word but a way of life. A person can be either merciful or unmerciful; it is a lifestyle. I choose to live in a way that is merciful or I choose to live in a way that is unmerciful. It is one thing to *speak* of mercy, and it is another to *live* mercy. Paraphrasing the words of St. James the Apostle (cf. 2:14–17), we could say: *mercy without works is dead within itself.* That's it! What makes mercy come alive is its constant dynamism in order to go and meet those in need and the necessities of those in spiritual and material hardship. Mercy has eyes to see, ears to hear, hands to lift up again...

Daily life allows us to touch, with our hands, the urgent needs experienced by the poorest and most tested of people. We are asked for a particular kind of attention that leads us to *notice* the state of suffering and need in which so many of our brothers and sisters find themselves. Sometimes we pass by situations of desperate poverty and seem to remain untouched. Life simply goes on, as if everything were fine, leading eventually to a state of indifference where we become hypocrites and, without our realizing it, succumb to a form of spiritual lethargy that numbs the soul and renders life barren. People who pass by, who move on in life without noticing the needs of others, without seeing the many spiritual and material needs of others, are people who pass by without living; they are people who do not serve others. Remember: those who do not live to serve, do not serve to live.

There are so many aspects of God's mercy toward us! In the same way, there are so many faces turned to us in order to obtain mercy. Those who have experienced in their own lives the Father's mercy cannot remain indifferent to the needs of their brothers and sisters. The lesson of Jesus that we have heard does not allow escape routes: I was hungry and you gave me food; I was thirsty and you gave me drink; I was naked, displaced, sick, in prison, and you assisted me (Mt 25:35–36). You cannot ignore a person who is hungry: he must be fed. Jesus tells us this! The works of mercy are not theoretical ideas but concrete acts of witness. They oblige us to roll up our sleeves to alleviate suffering.

Due to changes in our globalized world, certain material and spiritual forms of poverty have multiplied. Let us give space, therefore, to the imaginings of charity so as to find new ways of working. In this manner, the way of mercy will become more and more concrete. It is necessary that we remain as vigilant as watchmen, so that, when facing the poverty produced by the culture of wellbeing, the Christian gaze does not weaken and become incapable of focusing on what is essential. Focus on the essential. What does this mean? To focus on Jesus, to see Jesus in the hungry, in prisoners, in the sick, in the naked, in those who don't have work and need to care for their family. To see Jesus in these people, our brothers and sisters; to see Jesus in those who are lonely, or sad, in those who have made mistakes and need counsel, in those who need to walk with him in silence so that they feel accompanied. These are the works that Jesus asks of us! To see Jesus in them, in these people. Why? Because this is the way Jesus sees me, this is the way Jesus sees all of us.

—*General Audience, Saint Peter's Square, June 30, 2016*

TOUCHING THE FLESH OF CHRIST

Love is the highest expression of life; it allows us to exist! Before this essential truth of our faith, the Church can never allow herself to act as that priest and that Levite who ignored the man half dead by the side of the road (cf. Lk 10:25–36). She cannot look away and turn her back on the many forms of poverty that cry out for mercy. This turning one's back in order not to see hunger, sickness, exploited persons . . . this is a grave sin! It is also a modern sin, a sin of our times! We Christians cannot allow ourselves to do this. It is not worthy of the Church nor of any Christian to "pass by on the other side," and to pretend to have a clean conscience simply because we have said our prayers or because we have been to Mass on Sunday. No. Calvary is always real; it has not disappeared, nor does it remain with us merely as a nice painting in our churches. That culmination of compassion, from which the love of God flows to our human misery, still speaks to us today and spurs us on to offer ever new signs of mercy.

I will never tire of saying that the mercy of God is not some beautiful idea, but rather a concrete action. There is no mercy without concrete works. Mercy is not doing good "in passing," but getting involved where there is something wrong, where there is illness, where there is hunger, wherever there is exploitation. And even human mercy is not authentic—that is, human and merciful—until it has found tangible expression in the actions of our daily life. The warning of the apostle John has perennial value: "Little children, let us not love in word and speech but in deed and truth" (1 Jn 3:18). The truth of mercy is expressed in our daily gestures that make God's action visible in our midst.

Brothers and sisters, you represent the large and varied world of volunteer workers. You are among the most precious realities of the Church, you who every day, often silently and unassumingly, give shape and visibile form to mercy. You are *crafters of mercy*: with your hands, with your eyes, with your hearing, with your closeness, by your touch...artisans! You express one of the most noble desires of the human heart, making a suffering person feel loved. In the various contexts of need experienced by so many people, your presence is the hand of Christ held out to all, and reaching all. You are the hand of Christ held out. Have you thought about this? The credibility of the Church too is conveyed in a convincing way through your service to abandoned children, to the sick, to the poor who lack food or work, to the elderly, the homeless, prisoners, refugees and immigrants, to all struck by natural disasters...Indeed, wherever there is a cry for help, there your active and selfless witness is found. In bearing one another's burdens, you make Christ's law visible (cf. Gal 6:2; Jn 13:34).

Dear brothers and sisters, you touch the flesh of Christ with your hands. Do not forget this: you touch the flesh of Christ with your hands. Be always ready to offer solidarity, to be steadfast in your closeness to others, determined in awakening joy and genuine in giving comfort. The world stands in need of concrete signs of solidarity, especially as it is faced with the temptation to indifference. It requires persons who, by their lives, defy such individualism, which is the tendency to think only of oneself and to ignore the brother or sister in need. Be always happy and full of joy in the service you give, but never presume to think that you are superior to others. Instead, let your work of mercy be a humble and eloquent continuation of the presence of Jesus who continues to bend down to our level to take care of the ones who suffer. For love "builds up" (1 Cor 8:1), day after day helping our communities to be signs of fraternal communion.

I invite you all to pray in silence for the many, many people who suffer, for so much suffering, for all who are discarded by society. Pray also for the many volunteers like you, those who go out to encounter the flesh of Christ, to touch it, to care for it, to be close to it. And pray for the many, many who in the face of all this poverty simply turn their backs and who hear in their hearts a voice that says: "This does not affect me, this is not important to me." Let us pray in silence.

—*Catechesis for all workers of mercy and volunteers,*
Saint Peter's Square, September 3, 2016

II

THE CORPORAL
WORKS OF MERCY

BEARERS OF CHRIST

The Immaculate One has become the sublime icon of the divine mercy that conquered sin...In imitation of Mary, we are called to become bearers of Christ and witnesses to his love, looking first of all to those who are privileged in the eyes of Jesus. It is they who he himself indicated: "I was hungry and you gave me food, I was thirsty and you gave me drink, I was a stranger and you welcomed me, I was naked and you clothed me, I was sick and you visited me, I was in prison and you came to me" (Mt 25:35–36)...

One cannot understand a true Christian who is not merciful, just as one cannot comprehend God without his mercy. This is the epitomizing word of the Gospel: mercy. It is the fundamental feature of the face of Christ: that face that we recognize in the various aspects of his existence: when he goes to meet everyone, when he heals the sick, when he sits at the table with sinners, and above all when, nailed to the cross, he forgives; there we see the face of divine mercy.

— Angelus, *Solemnity of the Immaculate Conception,*
December 8, 2015

Feeding the Hungry

BEING SERVANTS

Today we celebrate, in addition to the feast of Saint Joseph, the beginning of the ministry of the new bishop of Rome, the successor of Peter, which also involves a certain power. Certainly, Jesus Christ conferred power upon Peter, but what sort of power was it? Jesus' three questions to Peter about love are followed by three commands: feed my lambs, tend my sheep, feed my sheep. Let us never forget that authentic power is service, and that the pope too, when exercising power, must enter ever more fully into that service which has its radiant culmination on the cross. He must be inspired by the lowly, concrete, and faithful service which marked Saint Joseph and, like him, he must open his arms to protect all of God's people and embrace with tender affection the whole of humanity, especially the poorest, the weakest, the least important, those whom Matthew lists in the final judgment on love: the hungry, the thirsty, the stranger, the naked, the sick, and those in prison (cf. Mt 25:31–46). Only those who serve with love are able to protect!

—*Homily, Mass for the Beginning of the Petrine Ministry,*
Saint Peter's Square, March 19, 2013

INCREASING INEQUITIES

In our time humanity is experiencing a turning point in its history, as we can see from the advances being made in so many fields. We can only praise the steps being taken to improve people's welfare in areas such as health care, education, and communications. At the same time we have to remember that the majority of our contemporaries are barely living from day to day, with dire consequences. A number of diseases are spreading. The hearts of many people are gripped by fear and desperation, even in the so-called rich countries. The joy of living frequently fades, lack of respect for others and violence are on the rise, and inequality is increasingly evident. It is a struggle to live and, often, to live with precious little dignity. This epochal change has been set in motion by the enormous qualitative, quantitative, rapid, and cumulative advances occurring in the sciences and in technology, and by their instant application in different areas of nature and of life. We are in an age of knowledge and information, which has led to new and often anonymous kinds of power.

—Evangelii Gaudium, 52

AN ECONOMY THAT KILLS

Just as the commandment "Thou shalt not kill" sets a clear limit in order to safeguard the value of human life, today we also have to say "Thou shalt not" to an economy of exclusion and inequality. Such an economy kills. How can it be that it is not a news item when an elderly homeless person dies of exposure, but it is news when the stock market loses two points? This is a case of exclusion. Can we continue to stand by when food is thrown away while people are starving? This is a case of inequality. Today everything comes under the laws of competition and the survival of the fittest, where the powerful feed upon the powerless. As a consequence, masses of people find themselves excluded and marginalized: without work, without possibilities, without any means of escape.

—Evangelii Gaudium, 53

NOT REMAINING DEAF

Each individual Christian and every community is called to be an instrument of God for the liberation and promotion of the poor, and for enabling them to be fully a part of society. This demands that we be docile and attentive to the cry of the poor and that we come to their aid. A mere glance at the scriptures is enough to make us see how our gracious Father wants to hear the cry of the poor: "I have observed the misery of my people who are in Egypt; I have heard their cry on account of their taskmasters. Indeed, I know their sufferings, and I have come down to deliver them...so I will send you..." (Ex 3:7–8, 10). We also see how he is concerned for their needs: "When the Israelites cried out to the Lord, the Lord raised up for them a deliverer" (Jg 3:15). If we, who are God's means of hearing the poor, turn deaf ears to this plea, we oppose the Father's will and his plan; that poor person "might cry to the Lord

33

against you, and you would incur guilt" (Dt 15:9). A lack of solidarity toward his or her needs will directly affect our relationship with God: "For if in bitterness of soul he calls down a curse upon you, his Creator will hear his prayer" (Sir 4:6). The old question always returns: "How does God's love abide in anyone who has the world's goods, and sees a brother or sister in need and yet refuses help?" (1 Jn 3:17). Let us recall also how bluntly the apostle James speaks of the cry of the oppressed: "The wages of the laborers who mowed your fields, which you kept back by fraud, cry out, and the cries of the harvesters have reached the ears of the Lord of hosts" (5:4).

—Evangelii Gaudium, *187*

A MISSION FOR ALL

The Church has realized that the need to heed the cry of the poor is itself born of the liberating action of grace within each of us, and thus it is not a question of a mission reserved only to a few: "The Church, guided by the Gospel of mercy and by love for mankind, hears the cry for justice and intends to respond to it with all her might" (*Libertatis Nuntius*, 903). In this context we can understand Jesus' command to his disciples: "You yourselves give them something to eat!" (Mk 6:37): it means working to eliminate the structural causes of poverty and to promote the integral development of the poor, as well as small daily acts of solidarity in meeting the real needs that we encounter. The word "solidarity" is a little worn and at times poorly understood, but it refers to something more than a few sporadic acts of generosity. It presumes the creation of a new mindset that thinks in terms of community and the priority of the life of all over the appropriation of goods by a few.

—Evangelii Gaudium, *188*

EDUCATING OURSELVES IN HUMANITY

It is a scandal that there is still hunger and malnutrition in the world! It is not just a question of responding to immediate emergencies, but of addressing together, at all levels, a problem that challenges our personal and social conscience, in order to achieve a just and lasting solution. May no one be obliged to abandon his or her country or own cultural environment due to a lack of essential means of subsistence! Paradoxically, in an age when globalization enables us to know about the situations of need that exist in the world and to multiply exchanges and human relationships, the tendency to individualism and to withdraw into ourselves seems to be on the rise. These tendencies lead to a certain attitude of indifference—at the personal, institutional and state level—toward those who are dying of hunger or suffering from malnutrition, almost as though it were an inevitable fact. However, hunger and malnutrition can never be considered a normal occurrence to which one must become accustomed, as if it were part of the system. Something has to change in ourselves, in our mentality, in our societies. What can we do? I think that an important step is to tear down decisively the barriers of individualism, self-withdrawal, and the slavery to profit at all costs, and this needs to be accomplished not only in the dynamics of human relations but also in global economic and financial dynamics. Today, more than ever, I think it is necessary *to educate ourselves in solidarity*, to rediscover the value and meaning of this very uncomfortable word, which oftentimes has been left aside, and to make it become a basic attitude in decisions made at the political, economic, and financial levels, in relationships between persons, peoples, and nations. It is only by standing firmly united, by overcoming selfish ways of thinking and partisan interests, that the objective of eliminating forms of indigence resulting from a lack of food will also be achieved. A solidarity that is not reduced to different forms of welfare, but that makes an effort to ensure that an ever greater number of persons are economically independent. Many steps have been taken in different countries, but we are still far from a world where all can live with dignity...

However, wasting food is only one of the fruits of the "culture of waste" that often lead to sacrificing men and women to the idols of profit and consumption. It is a sad sign of the "globalization of indifference" that slowly leads us to grow "accustomed" to the suffering of others, as though it were normal. The challenge of hunger and malnutrition does not only have an economic or scientific dimension that relates to the quantitative and qualitative aspects of the food supply chain; it also and above all has an ethical and anthropological dimension. To educate in solidarity therefore means *to educate ourselves in humanity*. To build a society that is truly human means to put the person and his or her dignity at the center, always, and never to sell him or her out to the logic of profit.

—*Message for World Food Day, 2013*

Changing the Paradigm

To defeat hunger, it is not enough to meet the needs of those who are less fortunate or to help through aid and donations those who live in situations of emergency. It is instead necessary to change the paradigm of aid and of development policies, to modify international laws regarding the production and trade of agricultural products, guaranteeing to countries in which agriculture represents the foundation of the economy and of survival the self-determination of their own agricultural market.

How long will we continue to defend systems of production and consumption that exclude most of the world's population even from the crumbs that fall from the tables of the rich? The time has come to think and decide, beginning with each person and community rather than with market trends. Therefore, there must also be a change in the concepts of work, goals, economic activity, food production, and environmental protection. This is perhaps the only possibility for building an authentic future of peace, which today is threatened by food insecurity.

—*Message for World Food Day, 2014*

How Are We Using the Earth's Resources?

The continuing disgrace of hunger in the world moves me to share with you the question: *How are we using the earth's resources?* Contemporary societies should reflect on the hierarchy of priorities to which production is directed. It is a truly pressing duty to use the earth's resources in such a way that all may be free from hunger. Initiatives and possible solutions are many, and they are not limited to an increase in production. It is well known that present production is sufficient, and yet millions of persons continue to suffer and die from hunger, and this is a real scandal. We need, then, to find ways by which all may benefit from the fruits of the earth, not only to avoid the widening gap between those who have more and those who must be content with the crumbs, but above all because it is a question of justice, equality, and respect for every human being. In this regard I would like to remind everyone of that necessary *universal destination of all goods* which is one of the fundamental principles of the Church's social teaching. Respect for this principle is the essential condition for facilitating an effective and fair access to those essential and primary goods that every person needs and to which he or she has a right.

—*Message for World Day of Peace, January 1, 2014*

SHARING WHAT WE HAVE

When the apostles said to Jesus that the people who had come to listen to his words were hungry, he invited them to go and look for food. Being poor themselves, all they found were five loaves and two fish. But, with the grace of God, they managed to feed a multitude of people—even managing to collect what was left over and avoiding its going to waste.

We face a global scandal of around one billion—one billion!—people who still suffer from hunger today. We cannot look the other way and pretend this does not exist. The loaves and fishes teach us exactly this lesson: that if there is the will, what we have never ends. On the contrary, what we have more than abounds and does not get wasted. Therefore, dear brothers and sisters, I invite you to make space in your heart for this emergency of respecting the God-given rights of everyone to have access to adequate food. We share what we have in Christian charity with those who face numerous obstacles to satisfy such a basic need. At the same time, we promote an authentic cooperation with the poor so that through the fruits of their and our work they can live a dignified life.

I invite all of the institutions of the world, the Church, and each of us, as one single human family, to give voice to all of those who suffer silently from hunger, so that this voice becomes a roar which can shake the world.

This campaign is also an invitation to all of us to become more conscious in our food choices, which often lead to waste and a poor use of the resources available to us. It is also a reminder to stop thinking that our daily actions do not have an impact on the lives of those who suffer from hunger...Let us pray that the Lord may give us the grace to envisage a world in which no one must ever again die of hunger.

—Video-message for the Campaign against World Hunger,
December 9, 2013

Dignity, Not Alms

Nowadays there is much talk of rights, frequently neglecting duties; perhaps we have paid too little heed to those who are hungry. It is also painful to see that the fight against hunger and malnutrition is hindered by "market priorities," and the "primacy of profit," which have reduced foodstuffs to a commodity like any other, subject to financial speculation. And when we speak of new rights, the hungry are there too, standing on the street corner, asking for the right to citizenship, asking for due consideration of their status, asking for their human right to adequate and healthy food. They ask for dignity, not for alms.

—Speech to the UN Food and Agriculture Organization,
November 20, 2014

A HUNGER FOR DIGNITY

Dear friends, it is certainly necessary to give bread to the hungry—this is an act of justice. But there is also a deeper hunger, the hunger for a happiness that only God can satisfy, the hunger for dignity. There is neither real promotion of the common good nor real human development when there is ignorance of the fundamental pillars that govern a nation, its non-material goods: *life*, which is a gift of God, a value always to be protected and promoted; the *family*, the foundation of coexistence and a remedy against social fragmentation; *integral education*, which cannot be reduced to the mere transmission of information for purposes of generating profit; *health*, which must seek the comprehensive well-being of the person, including the spiritual dimension, essential for human balance and healthy coexistence; *security*, in the conviction that violence can be overcome only by changing human hearts.

—Visit to the community of Varginha, Rio de Janeiro, Brazil,
July 25, 2013

CHANGING LIFESTYLES

Climate change rightly worries us, but we cannot overlook financial speculation: for example, the high prices of wheat, rice, corn, and soy, which fluctuate on the stock market. The prices are linked to profits; the higher the price the greater the profit. Here too, let us take a different path, agreeing that the produce of the land has a value that we might call "sacred," for it is the fruit of the daily labor of people, families, communities of farmers. It is a labor often dominated by uncertainty, concern about climatic conditions, anxiety over the possible destruction of the harvest...

We must begin from our daily routine if we want to change lifestyles, conscious that our small acts can ensure sustainability and the future of the human family.

—Address to the Food and Agriculture Commission, June 11, 2015

MAKING CHRIST PRESENT

After the multiplication of the loaves, the people went in search of Jesus and finally found him near Capernaum. He was well aware of the motive for their great enthusiasm in seeking him and he made this clear to them: "You seek me, not because you saw signs, but because you ate your fill of the loaves" (Jn 6:26). In fact, those people followed him for the material bread that had sated their hunger the previous day, when Jesus had performed the multiplication of the loaves. The people had not understood that that bread, broken for so many, for the multitude, was *the expression of the love* of Jesus himself...Jesus does not eliminate the concern and search for daily food. No, he does not remove the concern for all that can make life better. But Jesus reminds us that the true meaning of our earthly existence lies at the end, in eternity...Meeting and welcoming within us Jesus, the "Bread of Life," gives meaning and hope to the often winding journey of life. This "Bread of Life" is given to us with a task, namely, that we in our turn satisfy the spiritual and material hunger of our brothers, proclaiming the Gospel the world over. With the witness of our loving union with every one of our brothers and sisters, our solidarity with our neighbor, we render Christ and his love present amid all humanity.

—Angelus, *August 2, 2015*

CONCRETE GESTURES

In the spirit of the Jubilee of Mercy, all of us are called to realize how indifference can manifest itself in our lives and to work concretely to improve the world around us, beginning with our families, our neighbors, and our places of employment.

Civil society is likewise called to make specific and courageous gestures of concern for their most vulnerable members, such as prisoners, migrants, the unemployed, and the infirm...

In this Jubilee Year of Mercy, I would also appeal to national leaders for concrete gestures in favor of our brothers and sisters who suffer from the lack of *labor, land,* and *lodging.* I am thinking of the creation of dignified jobs to combat the social plague of unemployment, which affects many families and young people and has grave effects for society as a whole. Unemployment takes a heavy toll on people's sense of dignity and hope, and can be only partially compensated for by the welfare benefits, however necessary these may be, provided to the unemployed and their families. Special attention needs to be given to women—who unfortunately still encounter discrimination in the workplace—and to some categories of workers whose conditions are precarious or dangerous, and whose pay is not commensurate to the importance of their social mission.

—Message for World Day of Peace, 2016

Giving Drink to the Thirsty

Fresh drinking water is an issue of primary importance, since it is indispensable for human life and for supporting terrestrial and aquatic ecosystems. Sources of fresh water are necessary for health care, agriculture, and industry. Water supplies used to be relatively constant, but now in many places demand exceeds the sustainable supply, with dramatic consequences in the short and long term. Large cities dependent on significant supplies of water have experienced periods of shortage, and at critical moments these have not always been administered with sufficient oversight and impartiality. Water poverty especially affects Africa, where large sectors of the population have no access to safe drinking water or experience droughts that impede agricultural production. Some countries have areas rich in water while others endure drastic scarcity.

One particularly serious problem is the quality of water available to the poor. Every day, unsafe water results in many deaths and the spread of water-related diseases, including those caused by microorganisms and chemical substances. Dysentery and cholera, linked to inadequate hygiene and water supplies, are a significant cause of suffering and of infant mortality. Underground water sources in many places are threatened by the pollution produced by certain mining, farming, and industrial activities, especially in countries lacking adequate regulation or controls. It is not only a question of industrial waste. Detergents and chemical products, commonly used in many places of the world, continue to pour into our rivers, lakes, and seas.

—Laudato Si', *28—29*

ACCESS TO WATER

Even as the quality of available water is constantly diminishing, in some places there is a growing tendency, despite its scarcity, to privatize this resource, turning it into a commodity subject to the laws of the market. Yet *access to safe, drinkable water is a basic and universal human right, since it is essential to human survival and, as such, is a condition for the exercise of other human rights.* Our world has a grave social debt toward the poor who lack access to drinking water, because *they are denied the right to a life consistent with their inalienable dignity.* This debt can be paid partly by an increase in funding to provide clean water and sanitary services among the poor. But water continues to be wasted, not only in the developed world but also in developing countries that possess it in abundance. This shows that the problem of water is partly an educational and cultural issue, since there is little awareness of the seriousness of such behavior within a context of great inequality.

—Laudato Si', *30*

Basic Services

One very serious problem in [poor neighborhoods] is the lack of access to infrastructures and basic services. By this I mean toilets, sewers, drains, refuse collection, electricity, and roads, as well as schools, hospitals, recreational and sport centers, studios and workshops for artists and craftsmen. I refer in particular to access to drinking water... To deny a family water, under any bureaucratic pretext whatsoever, is a great injustice, especially when one profits from this need.

—*Visit to the Kangemi slum, Nairobi, Kenya, November 27, 2015*

Sister Water

Water is the most essential element for life, and the future of humanity depends on our capacity to guard it and share it. I therefore encourage the international community to be vigilant so as to ensure that the planet's waters are adequately protected and that no one is excluded or discriminated against in the use of this resource, which is a resource par excellence. With Saint Francis of Assisi, we say: "Praised be You, my Lord, through Sister Water, / she is very useful and humble and precious and pure" (*Canticle of the Sun*).

—Angelus, *March 22, 2015*

Clothing the Naked

The spirit of hypocrisy makes us forget how to cherish a sick person, a child, an old person. And it keeps us from looking into the eyes of someone when we give them alms and withdraw our hand at once so that it won't get dirty.

Isaiah speaks of the spirit of hypocrisy, of formalism in fulfilling God's commandments, in this case fasting..."Is not this the fast that I choose: to loose the bonds of injustice, to undo the thongs of the yoke, to let the oppressed go free, and to break every yoke? Is it not to share your bread with the hungry, and bring the homeless poor into your house; when you see the naked to cover them, and not hide yourself from your own kin?" Here is the true meaning of fasting. To care for your brother's life, not to be ashamed of your brother's flesh, as Isaiah himself says. In fact, our perfection, our holiness progresses with our people, among whom we are chosen and to whom we belong. And our greatest act of holiness lies in the body of our brother, and the body of Jesus Christ...

Thus, our act of holiness today—of us who are here before the altar—is not hypocritical fasting. It means not being ashamed of the body of Christ who comes to us here today. For this is the mystery of the body and blood of Christ: it means sharing our bread with the hungry, healing the sick, the old, those who can't give us anything in return: that's what not being ashamed of the body means.

God's salvation is for a people, a people that progresses, a people consisting of brothers and sisters who are not ashamed of one another. This is perhaps the most difficult fast: the fasting of kindness. This is where kindness brings us. For perhaps [in the story of the Good Samaritan], the priest who passed by on the other side of that wounded man thought, "If I touch his blood, that wounded flesh, I'll become unclean and I won't be able to keep the Sabbath!" He was ashamed of the body of that man. That's hypocrisy! On the other hand, when [the Samaritan] was passing and saw the wounded man, he saw his brother's body, the body of a man belonging to his people, a son of God like himself. And he wasn't ashamed.

"So today the church suggests a true and thorough examination of conscience... Am I ashamed of my brother's or my sister's body? When I give alms, do I drop the money without touching the person's hand?... When I give alms, do I look my brother or sister in the eye? When I know that someone is sick, do I go to them? Do I greet them warmly? Do I know how to touch with tenderness sick people, old people, children? Or have I lost the sense of what it means to cherish someone?

Hypocrites no longer know how to touch others with tenderness; they have forgotten how to do it. So that is the advice: not to be ashamed of our brother's flesh: it's our flesh. For we will be judged by our behavior toward that brother, that sister, and certainly not by hypocritical fasting.

—*Morning homily, March 7, 2014*

The Example of the Simple

Mother Church teaches us to give food and drink to those who are hungry and thirsty, to clothe those who are naked. And how does she do this? She does it through the example of so many saints, men and women, who did this in an exemplary fashion; but she does it also through the example of so many fathers and mothers who teach their children that what we have that is extra is for those who lack the basic necessities. It is important to know this. The rule of hospitality has always been sacred in the simplest Christian families: there is always a plate and a bed for the one in need.

—*General Audience, Saint Peter's Square, September 10, 2014*

Being Like Him

Today's gospel passage presents Jesus' encounter with the Samaritan woman in Sicar, near an old well where the woman went to draw water daily. That day she found Jesus seated, "wearied as he was with his journey" (Jn 4:6). He immediately said to her: "Give me a drink" (v. 7). In this way he overcame the barriers of hostility that existed between Jews and Samaritans and broke the mold of prejudice against women. This simple request from Jesus is the start of a frank dialogue through which he enters with great delicacy into the interior world of a person to whom, according to social norms, he should not have spoken. But Jesus does! Jesus is not afraid. When Jesus sees a person he goes ahead, because he loves. He loves us all. He never hesitates before a person out of prejudice. Jesus sets her own situation before her, not by judging her but by making her feel worthy, acknowledged, and thus arousing in her the desire to go beyond her daily routine.

Jesus' thirst was not so much for water, but for the encounter with a parched soul. Jesus needed to encounter the Samaritan woman in order to open her heart: he asks for a drink so as to bring to light her own thirst. The woman is moved by this encounter. She asks Jesus several profound questions that we all carry within us but often ignore. We, too, have many questions to ask, but we don't have the courage to ask Jesus! Lent, dear brothers and sisters, is an opportune time to look within ourselves, to understand our truest spiritual needs, and to ask the Lord's help in prayer. The example of the Samaritan woman invites us to exclaim: "Jesus, give me a drink that will quench my thirst forever" . . .

In this gospel passage we likewise find the impetus to "leave behind our water jar," the symbol of everything that is seemingly important but that loses all its value before the "love of God" . . . I ask you, and myself: "What is your interior water jar, the one that weighs you down, that distances you from God?" Let us set it aside a little and, with our hearts, let us hear the voice of Jesus offering us another kind of water, a water that brings us close to the Lord. We are called to rediscover the importance and the meaning of our Christian life that was initiated in baptism and, like the Samaritan woman, to witness to our brothers. A witness of what? Joy! To witness to the joy of the encounter with Jesus, for, as I said, every encounter with Jesus changes our life, and every encounter with Jesus also fills us with joy, the joy that comes from within. And the Lord is like this. And so we must tell of the marvelous things the Lord can do in our hearts when we have the courage to set aside our own water jar.

—Angelus, *March 23, 2014*

BEING WITH THE POOR

This place is a special place... Here Saint Francis divested himself of everything, before his father, before the bishop and the people of Assisi. It was a prophetic gesture, and it was also an act of prayer, an act of love for and of trust in the Father who is in Heaven.

With this gesture Francis made his choice: the choice to be poor. That was not a sociological, ideological choice; it was a choice to be like Jesus, to imitate him, to follow him to the end. Jesus is God stripped of his glory. We read in Saint Paul: Christ Jesus, who was in the form of God, stripped himself, and made himself like us, and in this humiliation came to die on a cross (cf. Phil 2:6–8). Jesus is God, but he was born naked, he was placed in a manger, and he died naked and crucified. Francis stripped himself of everything, of his worldly life, of himself, to follow his Lord,

Jesus, to be like him. Bishop Guido understood this act and immediately rose, embraced Francis, covered him with his cloak, and was ever after his helper and protector (cf. *Vita Prima, FF,* 344).

Saint Francis's act of renunciation tells us simply what the Gospel teaches: following Jesus means putting him in first place, stripping ourselves of the many things we possess that suffocate our hearts, renouncing ourselves, taking up the cross and carrying it with Jesus. It means stripping ourselves of prideful ego and detaching ourselves from the desire to possess, from money, which is an idol that possesses.

We are all called to be poor, to strip us of ourselves, and to do this we must learn how to be with the poor, to share with those who lack basic necessities, to touch the flesh of Christ! The Christian is not one who speaks about the poor. No! He is one who encounters them, who looks them in the eye, who touches them. I am here not to "make news," but to indicate that this is the Christian path, the path Saint Francis followed. Saint Bonaventure, speaking of Saint Francis's renunciation, writes: "Thus, then, the servant of the Most High King was left despoiled, that he might follow the Lord Whom he loved." And he adds that in this way Francis was saved from "the shipwreck of the world" (*FF* 1043).

But I would, as a pastor, ask myself as well: What should the Church strip herself of?

She must strip away every kind of worldly spirit, which is a temptation for everyone; strip away every action that is not for God, that is not from God; strip away the fear of opening the doors and going out to encounter all, especially the poorest of the poor, the needy, the isolated, without waiting. Certainly not to get lost in the shipwreck of the world, but to bear with courage the light of Christ, the light of the Gospel, even in the darkness, where one can't see, where one might stumble. She must strip away the seeming assurance provided by structures, which, though certainly necessary and important, should never obscure the one true strength she carries within her: God. He is our strength! To strip away what is not essential, because our reference is Christ; the Church is Christ's! Many steps, above all in recent decades, have been taken. Let us continue on this path, Christ's path, the path of saints.

—*Meeting with the poor assisted by Caritas, Assisi, October 4, 2013*

FORMS OF NAKEDNESS

To clothe the naked: what does it mean if not to restore dignity to one who has lost it? Certainly it means giving clothing to one who has none. But let us also think about the women victims of trafficking, cast onto the streets, or of other many ways of using the human body—even the bodies of minors—as a commodity. Likewise, not having a job, a house, a fair wage are forms of nakedness; being discriminated against on account of race, of faith, are all forms of "nakedness," to which as Christians we are called to be attentive, vigilant, and ready to act.

—*General Audience, Saint Peter's Square, October 26, 2016*

Welcoming the Stranger

REGAINING DIGNITY

*W*here *God is born, hope is born; and where hope is born, persons regain their dignity.* Yet even today great numbers of men and women are deprived of their human dignity and, like the child Jesus, suffer cold, poverty, and rejection. May our closeness today be felt by those who are most vulnerable, especially child soldiers, women who suffer violence, and the victims of human trafficking and the drug trade.

May we never withhold our compassion from those fleeing extreme poverty or war, traveling all too often in inhumane conditions and not infrequently at the risk of their lives. May God repay all those, both individuals and states, who generously work to provide assistance and welcome to the numerous migrants and refugees, helping them to build a dignified future for themselves and for their dear ones, and to be integrated into the societies that receive them.

On this festal day may the Lord grant renewed hope to all those who lack employment—and they are so many! May he sustain the commitment of those with public responsibilities in political and economic life, that they may work to pursue the common good and to protect the dignity of every human life.

—Urbi et Orbi *Message, Christmas 2015*

An Ocean of Mercy

Sometimes we ask ourselves how it is possible that human injustice persists unabated, and that the arrogance of the powerful continues to demean the weak, relegating them to the most squalid outskirts of our world. We ask how long human evil will continue to sow violence and hatred in our world, reaping innocent victims. How can the fullness of time have come when we are witnessing hordes of men, women, and children fleeing war, hunger, and persecution, ready to risk their lives simply to find respect for their fundamental rights? A torrent of misery, swollen by sin, seems to contradict the fullness of time brought by Christ... How do we explain this?... Even children are aware of this.

And yet this swollen torrent is powerless before the *ocean of mercy* that floods our world. All of us are called to immerse ourselves in this ocean, to let ourselves be reborn, to overcome the indifference that blocks solidarity, and to leave behind the false neutrality that prevents sharing. The grace of Christ, which brings our hope of salvation to fulfillment, leads us to cooperate with him in building an ever more just and fraternal world, a world in which every person and every creature can dwell in peace, in the harmony of God's original creation.

—*Homily at Mass for the closing of the International Congress of the* Pueri Cantores, *Vatican Basilica, January 1, 2016*

LIVING HOSPITALITY

Jesus calls his disciples and sends them out, giving them clear and precise instructions. He challenges them to take on a whole range of attitudes and ways of acting. Sometimes these can strike us as exaggerated or even absurd. It would be easier to interpret these attitudes symbolically or "spiritually." But Jesus is quite precise, very clear. He doesn't tell his disciples simply to do whatever they think they can.

Let us consider some of these attitudes: "Take nothing for the journey except a staff; no bread, no bag, no money…" "When you enter a house, stay there until you leave the place" (cf. Mk 6:8–11). All this might seem quite unrealistic.

We could concentrate on the words, "bread," "money," "bag," "staff," "sandals," and "tunic." And this would be fine. But it strikes me that one key word can easily pass unnoticed among the challenging words I have just listed. It is a word at the heart of Christian spirituality, of our experience of discipleship: "welcome." Jesus as the good master, the good teacher, sends them out to be welcomed, to experience hospitality. He says to them: "When you enter a house, stay there." He sends them out to learn one of the hallmarks of the community of believers. We might say that a Christian is someone who has learned to welcome others, who has learned to show hospitality.

Jesus does not send his disciples out as men of influence, landlords, officials armed with rules and regulations. Instead, he makes them see that the Christian journey is simply about changing hearts—one's own heart first all, and then helping to transform the hearts of others. It is about learning to live differently, under a different law, with different rules. It is about turning from the path of selfishness, conflict, division, and superiority, and taking instead the path of life, generosity, and love. It is about passing from a mentality that dominates, stifles, and manipulates to a mentality that welcomes, accepts, and cares.

These are two contrasting mentalities, two ways of approaching our life and our mission.

How many times do we see mission in terms of plans and programs? How many times do we see evangelization as involving any number of strategies, tactics, maneuvers, techniques—as if we could convert people on the basis of our own arguments? Today the Lord says to us quite clearly: in the mentality of the Gospel, you do not convince people with arguments, strategies, or tactics. You convince them by simply learning how to welcome them.

The Church is a mother with an open heart. She knows how to welcome and accept, especially those in need of greater care, those in greater difficulty. The Church, as envisioned by Jesus, is the home of hospitality. And how much good we can do, if only we try to speak this language of hospitality, this language of receiving and welcoming. How much pain can be soothed, how much despair can be allayed in a place where we feel at home! This requires open doors, especially the doors of our heart. Welcoming the hungry, the thirsty, the stranger, the naked, the sick, the prisoner (Mt 25:34–37), the leper, and the paralytic. Welcoming those who do not think as we do, who do not have faith or who have lost it—sometimes through our fault. Welcoming the persecuted, the unemployed.

Welcoming the different cultures with which our world is so richly blessed. Welcoming sinners, because each one of us is also a sinner.

So often we forget that there is an evil underlying our sins, that precedes our sins. There is a bitter root that causes damage, great damage, and silently destroys so many lives. There is an evil that, bit by bit, finds a place in our hearts and eats away at our life: it is isolation, an isolation that can have many roots, many causes. How much it destroys our life and how much harm it does to us. It makes us turn our back on others, God, the community. It makes us closed in on ourselves. Thus we can see that the real work of the Church, our mother, should not be mainly about managing works and projects, but rather about learning to experience fraternity with others. A welcoming fraternity is the best witness that God is our Father, for "by this all will know that you are my disciples, if you have love for one another" (Jn 13:35).

In this way, Jesus teaches us a new way of thinking and shows us a horizon brimming with life, beauty, truth, and fulfillment.

God never closes off horizons. He is never unconcerned about the lives and sufferings of his children. God never allows himself to be outdone in generosity. So he sends us his Son, he gives him to us, he hands him over, he shares him . . . so that we can learn the way of fraternity, of self-giving. In a definitive way, he opens up a new horizon. He is a new word that sheds light on so many situations of exclusion, disintegration, loneliness, and isolation. He is a word that breaks the silence of loneliness.

And when we are weary or worn down by our efforts to evangelize, it is good to remember that the life that Jesus holds out to us responds to the deepest needs of people. "We were created for what the Gospel offers us: friendship with Jesus and love of our brothers and sisters" (*Evangelii Gaudium*, 265).

One thing is sure: we cannot force anyone to receive us, to welcome us. This is itself part of our poverty and freedom. But neither can anyone force us not to be welcoming, open to the lives of our people. No one can tell us not to accept and embrace the lives of our brothers and sisters, especially those who have lost hope and enthusiasm for life. How good it would be to think of our parishes, communities, chapels— wherever there are Christians—not with closed doors but as true centers of encounter between ourselves and God.

The Church is a mother, like Mary. In her, we have a model. We too must provide a home, like Mary, who did not lord it over the word of God, but rather welcomed that word, bore it in her womb, and gave it to others.

We too must provide a home, like the earth, which does not choke the seed but receives it, nourishes it, and helps it grow.

That is how we want to be Christians. That is how we want to live the faith on this Paraguayan soil, like Mary, accepting and welcoming God's life in our brothers and sisters, in confidence and with the certainty that "the Lord will shower down blessings, and our land will yield its increase." May it be so.

—*Homily, Mass in Campo Grande, Asunción, Paraguay,*
July 12, 2015

The Light of Hope

The Church is mother and her maternal attention is expressed with special tenderness for and closeness to those who are obliged to flee their own country and exist between rootlessness and integration. This tension destroys people. Christian compassion—"suffering with" compassion—is expressed first of all in the commitment to learn about the events that force people to leave their homeland, and, where necessary, to give voice to those who cannot manage to make their cry of distress and oppression heard. By doing this you carry out an important task in sensitizing Christian communities to the multitudes of their brethren scarred by wounds that mark their existence: violence, abuse, the distance from family affection, traumatic events, flight from home, uncertainty about the future in refugee camps. These are all elements that dehumanize and must spur every Christian and the whole community to practical concern.

Today, however, dear friends, I would like to ask you all to see also a ray of hope in the eyes and hearts of refugees and of those who have been forcibly displaced, a hope that is expressed in expectations for the future, in the desire for friendship, in the wish to participate in the host society through learning its language, access to employment, and the education of children. I admire the courage of those who hope to be able gradually to resume a normal life, waiting for joy and love to return to brighten their existence. We can and must all nourish this hope!

Above all, I ask leaders and legislators and the entire international community to confront the reality of those who have been forcefully uprooted, to devise effective projects and new approaches in order to protect their dignity, to improve their quality of life, and to address the challenges that are emerging in modern forms of persecution, oppression, and slavery.

They are human people, I stress this, who are appealing for solidarity and assistance, who need urgent action but also and above all understanding and kindness. God is good; let us imitate God. Their condition cannot leave us indifferent. Moreover, as Church we should remember that in tending the wounds of refugees, evacuees, and the victims of trafficking, we are putting into practice the commandment of love that Jesus bequeathed to us when he identified with the foreigner, with those who are suffering, with all the innocent victims of violence and exploitation. We should reread more often chapter 25 of the Gospel according to Matthew in which he speaks of the last judgment (cf. vv. 31–46). And here I would also like to remind you of the attention that every pastor and Christian community must pay to the journey of faith of Christian refugees and Christians displaced by force, as well as of Christian emigrants. These people need special pastoral care that respects their traditions and accompanies them to harmonious integration with the ecclesial situations in which they find themselves. May our Christian communities really be places of hospitality, listening, and communion!

Dear friends, let us not forget the flesh of Christ is in the flesh of refugees: their flesh is the flesh of Christ. It is also your task to direct all the institutions working in the area of forced migration to new forms of co-responsibility. Unfortunately, the phenomenon of forced migration is growing. This makes your task increasingly demanding as you strive to promote tangible responses of closeness and support with people, taking into account their different local backgrounds.

— Address to the Pontifical Council for the Pastoral Care
of Migrants and Itinerant People, May 24, 2013

A Lesson in Solidarity

From the moment I first set foot on Brazilian soil, right up to this meeting here with you, I have been made to feel welcome. And it is important to be able to make people welcome. It is something even more beautiful than any kind of ornament or decoration. I say this because when we are generous in welcoming people and sharing something with them—some food, a place in our homes, our time—not only do we no longer remain poor: we are enriched. I am well aware that when someone needing food knocks at your door, you always find a way of sharing food. As the proverb says, one can always "add more water to the beans"! Is it possible to add more water to the beans?... Always?... And you do so with love, demonstrating that true riches are found not in material things, but in the heart!

And the Brazilian people, particularly the humblest among you, can offer the world a valuable lesson in solidarity. This word "solidarity" is too often forgotten or silenced, because it is uncomfortable. It almost seems like a bad word..."solidarity." I would like to make an appeal to those in possession of greater resources, to public authorities and to all people of good will who are working for social justice:

never tire of working for a more just world, marked by greater solidarity! No one can remain insensitive to the inequalities that persist in the world! Everybody, according to his or her particular opportunities and responsibilities, should be able to make a personal contribution to putting an end to so many social injustices. The culture of selfishness and individualism that often prevails in our society is not, I repeat, not what builds up and leads to a more habitable world. Rather, it is the culture of solidarity that does so. The culture of solidarity means seeing others not as rivals or statistics, but brothers and sisters. And we are all brothers and sisters!

— Address to the community of Varginha, Rio de Janeiro, Brazil,
July 25, 2013

HIDDEN EXILES

Joseph, Mary, and Jesus experienced the tragic fate of refugees, which is marked by fear, uncertainty, and unease (cf. Mt 2:13–15; 19–23). Unfortunately, in our own time, millions of families can identify with this sad reality. Almost every day the television and papers carry news of refugees fleeing from hunger, war, and other grave dangers, in search of security and a dignified life for themselves and for their families.

In distant lands, even when they find work, refugees and immigrants do not always find a true welcome, respect, or appreciation for the values they bring. Their legitimate expectations collide with complex and difficult situations that at times seem insurmountable. Therefore, as we fix our gaze on the Holy Family of Nazareth when they were forced to become refugees, let us think of the tragedy of the migrants and refugees who are victims of rejection and exploitation, who are victims of human trafficking and of slave labor. But let us also think of other "exiles." I would call them "hidden exiles," those exiles who can be found within their own families: the elderly, for example, who are sometimes treated as a burdensome presence. I often think that a good indicator for knowing how a family is doing is seeing how their children and elderly are treated.

Jesus wanted to belong to a family that experienced these hardships, so that no one would feel excluded from the loving closeness of God. The flight into Egypt caused by Herod's threat shows us that God is present where man is in danger, where man is suffering, where he is fleeing, where he experiences rejection and abandonment; but God is also present where man dreams, where he hopes to return in freedom to his homeland and plans and chooses life for his family and dignity for himself and his loved ones.

—Angelus, *December 29, 2013*

COME TO ME

Jesus himself sought out the tired, worn out crowds like sheep without a shepherd (cf. Mt 9:35–36), and he sought them out to proclaim to them the Kingdom of God and to heal many of them in body and spirit. Now he calls them all to himself: "Come to me," and he promises them relief and rest.

This invitation of Jesus reaches to our day and extends to the many brothers and sisters oppressed by life's precarious conditions, by existential and difficult situations that at times lack valid points of reference. In the poorest countries, but also on the outskirts of the richest countries, there are so many weary people, worn out under the unbearable weight of neglect and indifference. Indifference: human indifference causes the needy so much pain! And worse, the indifference of Christians! On the fringes of society so many men and women are tried by indigence, but also by dissatisfaction with life and by frustration. So many are forced to emigrate from their homeland, risking their lives. Many more, every day, carry the weight of an economic system that exploits human beings, imposing on them an unbearable "yoke," which the few privileged do not want to bear. To each of these children of the Father in heaven, Jesus repeats: "Come to me, all of you." But he also says it to those who have everything, but whose heart is empty and without God. Even to them, Jesus addresses this invitation: "Come to me." Jesus' invitation is for everyone, but especially for those who suffer the most.

Jesus promises to give rest to everyone, but he also gives us an invitation, which is like a commandment: "Take my yoke upon you, and learn from me; for I am gentle and lowly in heart" (Mt 11:29). The "yoke" of the Lord consists in taking on the burden of others with fraternal love. Once Christ's comfort and rest is received, we are called in turn to become rest and comfort for our brothers and sisters, with a docile and humble attitude, in imitation of the Teacher.

—Angelus, *July 6, 2014*

LIKE THE LEAVEN IN THE DOUGH

Afflictions and tribulations have not been lacking recently in the Middle East. They have been aggravated in the past few months because of the continuing hostilities in the region, but especially because of the work of a new and disturbing terrorist organization, with previously unimaginable characteristics, that has perpetrated all kinds of abuses and inhuman acts. It has particularly affected a number of you, who have been brutally driven out of your native lands, where Christians have been present since apostolic times.

Nor, in writing to you, can I remain silent about the members of other religious and ethnic groups who are also experiencing persecution and the effects of these conflicts. Every day I follow the news reports of the enormous suffering endured by many people in the Middle East. I think in particular of the children, the young mothers, the elderly, the homeless, and all refugees, the starving and those facing the prospect of a hard winter without adequate shelter. This suffering cries out to God and it calls for our commitment to prayer and concrete efforts to help in any way possible. I want to express to all of you my personal closeness and solidarity, as well as that of the whole Church, and to offer you a word of consolation and hope...

The situation in which are you living is a powerful summons to holiness of life, as saints and martyrs of every Christian community have attested. I think with affection and veneration of the pastors and faithful who have recently been killed, often merely because they were Christians. I think also of those who have been kidnapped, including several Orthodox bishops and priests of various rites. May they soon return, safe and sound, to their homes and communities! I ask God to grant that all this suffering united to the Lord's cross will bring about much good for the Church and for all the peoples in the Middle East.

In the midst of hostility and conflicts, the communion you experience in fraternity and simplicity is a sign of God's Kingdom. I am gratified by the good relations and cooperation that exist between the patriarchs of the Eastern Catholic churches and those of the Orthodox churches, and also between the faithful of the different churches. The sufferings that Christians endure contribute immensely to the cause of unity. It is the ecumenism of blood, which demands a trusting abandonment to the workings of the Holy Spirit.

May you always bear witness to Jesus amid your difficulties! Your very presence is precious for the Middle East. You are a small flock, but one with a great responsibility in the land where Christianity was born and first spread. You are like leaven in the dough. Even more than the many contributions that the Church makes in the areas of education, health care, and social services, which are esteemed by all, the greatest source of enrichment in the region is the presence of Christians themselves, your presence. Thank you for your perseverance!

—*Letter to Christians of the Middle East, December 21, 2014*

The Lord Passes

The example of Mary and Joseph is for us all an invitation to accept, with total openness of spirit, Jesus, who for love made himself our brother. He comes to bring to the world the gift of peace: "On earth peace among men with whom he is pleased" (Lk 2:14), as the choirs of angels proclaimed to the shepherds. The precious gift of Christmas is peace, and Christ is our true peace. And Christ speaks to our hearts to grant us peace, peace of soul. Let us open our doors to Christ!

—Angelus, *December 21, 2014*

OUR BROTHERS AND SISTERS

A boat full of migrants capsized last night about sixty miles off the Libyan coast and hundreds are feared dead. I express my deepest sorrow in the face of this tragedy and I assure for those lost and their families my remembrance in prayer. I address an urgent appeal that the international community will act decisively and and promptly to prevent any such tragedy from happening again. These were men and women like us, our brothers and sisters seeking a better life, starving, persecuted, wounded, exploited, victims of war. They were seeking a better life. They were seeking happiness... I invite you to pray in silence, first, and then all together for these brothers and sisters.

—Regina Coeli, *April 19, 2015*

CREATIVITY

Lack of housing is a grave problem in many parts of the world, both in rural areas and in large cities, since state budgets usually cover only a small portion of the demand. Not only the poor, but many other members of society as well find it difficult to own a home. Having a home has much to do with a sense of personal dignity and the growth of families.

This is a major issue for human ecology. In some places, where makeshift shantytowns have sprung up, this will mean developing those neighborhoods rather than razing or displacing them. When the poor live in unsanitary slums or in dangerous tenements, "in cases where it is necessary to relocate them, in order not to heap suffering upon suffering, adequate information needs to be given beforehand, with choices of decent housing offered, and the people directly involved must be part of the process" (Pontifical Council on Justice and Peace).

At the same time, creativity should be shown in integrating rundown neighborhoods into a welcoming city: "How beautiful those cities which overcome paralyzing mistrust, integrate those who are different, and make this very integration a new factor of development! How attractive are those cities which, even in their architectural design, are full of spaces which connect, relate and favor the recognition of others!" (*Evangelii Gaudium,* 210).

—Laudato Si', 152

A CALL

Faced with the tragedy of tens of thousands of refugees who flee death from war and hunger, and who have begun a journey moved by hope for survival, the Gospel calls us to be "neighbors" of the smallest and the most abandoned, and to give them concrete hope. It is not enough to say, "Take heart. Be patient" . . . Christian hope has a fighting spirit, with the tenacity of one who goes toward a sure goal.

Therefore, as the Jubilee of Mercy approaches, I make an appeal to parishes, religious communities, monasteries, and shrines throughout Europe, that they express the Gospel in a concrete way and host a refugee family. A practical gesture in preparation for the Holy Year of Mercy. May every parish, every religious community, every monastery, every shrine of Europe welcome one family, beginning with my Diocese of Rome.

I address my brother bishops of Europe, true pastors, that in their dioceses they may endorse my appeal, remembering that Mercy is the second name of Love: *"What you have done for the least of my brothers, that you have done for me"* (cf. Mt 25:46).

In the coming days, the two parishes of the Vatican will also welcome two families of refugees.

—Angelus, *September 6, 2015*

ENCOURAGEMENT

The Church in the United States knows like few others the hopes present in the hearts of immigrants. From the beginning you have learned their languages, promoted their cause, made their contributions your own, defended their rights, helped them to prosper, and kept alive the flame of their faith. Even today, no American institution does more for immigrants than your Christian communities. Now you are facing a stream of Latin immigration that affects many of your dioceses. Not only as the bishop of Rome, but also as a pastor from the South, I feel the need to thank and encourage you. Perhaps it will not be easy for you to look into their soul; perhaps you will be challenged by their diversity. But know that they also possess resources meant to be shared. So do not be afraid to welcome them. Offer them the warmth of the love of Christ and you will unlock the mystery of their heart. I am certain that, as so often in the past, these people will enrich America and its church.

—*Speech to Bishops of the United States, Washington, DC,*
September 23, 2015

The Golden Rule

In recent centuries, millions of people came to this land to pursue their dream of building a future in freedom. We, the people of this continent, are not fearful of foreigners, because most of us were once foreigners. I say this to you as the son of immigrants, knowing that so many of you are also descended from immigrants. Tragically, the rights of those who were here long before us were not always respected. For those peoples and their nations, from the heart of American democracy, I wish to reaffirm my highest esteem and appreciation. Those first contacts were often turbulent and violent, but it is difficult to judge the past by the criteria of the present. Nonetheless, when the stranger in our midst appeals to us, we must not repeat the sins and the errors of the past. We must resolve now to live as nobly and as justly as possible, as we educate new generations not to turn their back on our "neighbors" and everything around us. Building a nation calls us to recognize that we must constantly relate to others, rejecting a mindset of hostility in order to adopt one of reciprocal subsidiarity, in a constant effort to do our best. I am confident that we can do this.

Our world is facing a refugee crisis of a magnitude not seen since the Second World War. This presents us with great challenges and many hard decisions. On this continent, too, thousands of persons are led to travel north in search of a better life for themselves and for their loved ones, in search of greater opportunities. Is this not what we want for our own children? We must not be taken aback by their numbers, but rather view them as persons, seeing their faces and listening to their stories, trying to respond as best we can to their situation—to respond in a way that is always humane, just, and fraternal. We need to avoid a common temptation nowadays: to discard whatever proves troublesome. Let us remember the Golden Rule: "Do unto others as you would have them do unto you" (Mt 7:12).

This rule points us in a clear direction. Let us treat others with the same passion and compassion with which we want to be treated. Let us seek for others the same possibilities that we seek for ourselves. Let us help others to grow, as we would like to be helped ourselves. In a word, if we want security, let us give security; if we want life, let us give life; if we want opportunities, let us provide opportunities. The yardstick we use for others will be the yardstick that time will use for us.

—*Speech before Joint Session of Congress, Washington, DC,*
September 24, 2015

No Room in the Inn

The Bible is very clear: there was no room at the inn. I can imagine Joseph, with his wife about to have a child, with no shelter, no home, no place to stay. The Son of God came into this world as a homeless person. The Son of God knew what it was to start life without a roof over his head. We can imagine what Joseph must have been thinking. How is it that the Son of God has no home? Why are we homeless? Why don't we have housing? These are questions that many of you may ask, and do ask, every day. Like Saint Joseph, you may ask: Why are we homeless, without a place to live? And those of us who do have a home, a roof over our heads, would also do well to ask: Why do these, our brothers and sisters, have no place to live? Why are these brothers and sisters of ours homeless?

Joseph's questions are timely even today; they accompany all those who throughout history have been, and are, homeless.

Joseph was someone who asked questions. But, first and foremost, he was a man of faith. Faith gave Joseph the power to find light just at the moment when everything seemed dark. Faith sustained him amid the troubles of life. Thanks to faith, Joseph was able to press forward when everything seemed to be holding him back.

In the face of unjust and painful situations, faith brings us the light that scatters the darkness. As it did for Joseph, faith makes us open to the quiet presence of God at every moment of our lives, in every person and in every situation. God is present in every one of you, in each one of us.

I want to be very clear. There is no social or moral justi-fication, no justification whatsoever, for lack of housing. There are many unjust situations, but we know that God is suffering with us, experiencing them at our side. He does not abandon us.

—Visit with the homeless at Saint Patrick's parish, Washington, DC,
September 24, 2015

ACTING ON THE CAUSES

There needs to be a united response to the question of mi-gration. We cannot allow the Mediterranean to become a vast cemetery! The boats landing daily on the shores of Europe are filled with men and women who need accept-ance and assistance. The absence of mutual support within the European Union runs the risk of encouraging particu-laristic solutions to the problem, solutions that fail to take into account the human dignity of immigrants and thus contribute to slave labor and continuing social tensions.

Europe will be able to confront the problems associated with immigration only if it is capable of clearly asserting its own cultural identity and enacting adequate legislation to protect the rights of European citizens and ensure the ac-ceptance of immigrants; only if it is capable of adopting fair, courageous, and realistic policies that can assist the coun-tries of origin in their own social and political development and in their efforts to resolve internal conflicts—the princi-pal cause of this phenomenon—rather than adopting poli-cies motivated by self-interest, which increase and feed such conflicts.

We need to take action against the causes and not only the effects.

—Address to European Parliament, Strasburg, November 25, 2015

A Particular Challenge

It is essential to draw near to new forms of poverty and vulnerability, in which we are called to recognize the suffering Christ, even if this appears to bring us no tangible and immediate benefits. I think of the homeless, the addicted, refugees, indigenous peoples, the elderly who are increasingly isolated and abandoned, and many others. Migrants present a particular challenge for me, since I am the pastor of a Church without frontiers, a Church that considers herself mother to all. For this reason, I exhort all countries to a generous openness which, rather than fearing the loss of local identity, will prove capable of creating new forms of cultural synthesis. How beautiful are those cities that overcome paralyzing mistrust, integrate those who are different, and make this very integration a new factor of development! How attractive are those cities which, even in their architectural design, are full of spaces that connect, relate to, and favor the recognition of others!

—Evangelii Gaudium, 210

In Search of a Better Life

In our time, migration is growing worldwide. Refugees and people fleeing from their homes challenge individuals and communities and their traditional ways of life; at times they upset the cultural and social horizons they encounter. Increasingly, the victims of violence and poverty leaving their homelands are exploited by human traffickers during their journey toward the dream of a better future. If they survive the abuses and hardships of the journey, they then have to face latent suspicions and fear. In the end, they frequently encounter a lack of clear and practical policies regulating the acceptance of migrants and providing for short- or long-term programs of integration respectful of the rights and duties of all. Today, more than in the past, the Gospel of mercy troubles our consciences, prevents us from taking the suffering of others for granted, and points out a way of responding which, grounded in the theological virtues of faith, hope, and charity, finds practical expression in works of spiritual and corporal mercy...

Migrants are our brothers and sisters in search of a better life, far away from poverty, hunger, exploitation, and the unjust distribution of the planet's resources that are meant to be equitably shared by all. Don't we all want a better, more decent, and prosperous life to share with our loved ones?...

Biblical revelation urges us to welcome the stranger. It tells us that in so doing we open our doors to God, and that in the faces of others we see the face of Christ himself. Many institutions, associations, movements and groups as well as diocesan, national, and international organizations are experiencing the wonder and joy of the feast of encounter, sharing, and solidarity. They have heard the voice of Jesus Christ: "Behold, I stand at the door and knock" (Rev 3:20). Yet there continue to be debates about the conditions and limits to be set for the reception of migrants, not only on the level of national policies, but also in some parish communities whose traditional tranquility seems to be threatened.

Faced with these issues, how can the Church fail to be inspired by the example and words of Jesus Christ? The answer of the Gospel is mercy.

—*Message for the World Day of Refugees and Migrants 2016,*
January 17, 2016

OUR HEARTS DESIRE MORE

What is involved in the creation of "a better world"? The expression does not allude naively to abstract notions or unattainable ideals. Rather, it aims at an authentic and integral development, at efforts to provide dignified living conditions for everyone, at finding just responses to the needs of individuals and families, and at ensuring that God's gift of creation is respected, safeguarded, and cultivated. The Venerable Paul VI described the aspirations of people today in this way: "to secure a sure food supply, cures for diseases and steady employment . . . to exercise greater personal responsibility; to do more, to learn more, and have more, in order to be more" (*Populorum Progressio*, 6).

Our hearts do desire something "more." Beyond greater knowledge or possessions, they want to "be" more. Development cannot be reduced to economic growth alone, often attained without a thought for the poor and the vulnerable. A better world will come about only if attention is first paid to individuals; if human promotion is integral, taking account of every dimension of the person, including the spiritual; if no one is neglected, including the poor, the sick, prisoners, the needy, and the stranger (cf. Mt 25:31–46); if we can prove capable of leaving behind a throwaway culture and embracing one of encounter and acceptance.

Migrants and refugees are not pawns on the chessboard of humanity. They are children, women, and men who leave or who are forced to leave their homes for various reasons, who share a legitimate desire for knowing and having, but above all for being more.

—*Message for the World Day of Refugees and Migrants 2014,*
August 5, 2013

THE IMAGE OF CHRIST

Not infrequently, the arrival of migrants, displaced persons, asylum-seekers and refugees gives rise to suspicion and hostility. There is a fear that society will become less secure, that identity and culture will be lost, that competition for jobs will become stiffer, and even that criminal activity will increase. The communications media have a role of great responsibility in this regard. It is up to them, in fact, to break down stereotypes and to offer correct information in reporting the errors of a few as well as the honesty, rectitude, and goodness of the majority. A change of attitude toward migrants and refugees is needed on the part of everyone, moving away from attitudes of defensiveness and fear, indifference and marginalization—all typical of a throwaway culture—toward attitudes based on a culture of encounter, the only culture capable of building a better, more just, and fraternal world...

Every human being is a child of God! He or she bears the image of Christ! We ourselves need to see, and then to enable others to see, that migrants and refugees do not only represent a problem to be solved, but are brothers and sisters to be welcomed, respected, and loved. They are an occasion that Providence gives us to help build a more just society, a more perfect democracy, a more united country, a more fraternal world, and a more open and evangelical Christian community. Migration can offer possibilities for a new evangelization, open vistas for the growth of a new humanity foreshadowed in the paschal mystery, a humanity for which every foreign country is a homeland and every homeland is a foreign country.

Dear migrants and refugees! Never lose the hope that you too will find a more secure future, that on your journey you will encounter an outstretched hand, and that you can experience fraternal solidarity and the warmth of friendship! To all of you, and to those who have devoted their lives and their efforts to helping you, I give the assurance of my prayers and I cordially impart my Apostolic Blessing.

—Message for the World Day of Refugees and Migrants 2014,
August 5, 2013

A Little Story

Several days ago, a little story took place in the city. There was a refugee who was looking for a street and a lady approached him and said: "Are you looking for something?" The refugee, who had no shoes, answered: "I would like to go to Saint Peter's to enter the Holy Door." And the lady said to herself: "But he has no shoes, how will he manage to walk there?" So she got a taxi. But the migrant, that refugee, had a disagreeable odor and the taxi driver almost didn't want him to get in his car. In the end, however, he agreed to take the refugee. The lady, sitting next to him during the ride, asked him a little about his history as a refugee and migrant: it took ten minutes to get to Saint Peter's. This man told his story of suffering, war, and hunger because he had fled from his homeland in order to migrate here. After they arrived at Saint Peter's, when the lady opened her purse to pay for the ride, the taxi driver—who at first had not wanted the refugee in his taxi because he smelled—told her: "No, ma'am, I should be paying you because you made me listen to a story that has changed my heart." This lady knew what a migrant's pain is, because she was of Armenian descent and had known the suffering of her people. When we do something like this, at first we refuse because it causes us a little inconvenience: "but...he smells..." In the end, the episode gives fragrance to our soul and changes us. Consider this story and let us think about what we can do for refugees.

—*General Audience, Saint Peter's Square, October 26, 2016*

Visiting the Sick

With this work of mercy, the Lord invites us to do an act of great humanity: *sharing*. Let us remember this word: sharing. Those who are sick often feel alone. We cannot hide the fact that, especially in our days, in sickness one experiences greater loneliness than at other times in life. A visit can make a person who is sick feel less alone, and a little companionship is great medicine! A smile, a caress, a handshake are simple gestures, but they are very important for those who feel abandoned. How many people dedicate themselves to visiting the sick in hospitals or in their homes! It is priceless volunteer work. When it is done in the Lord's name, moreover, it also becomes an *eloquent and effective expression of mercy*. Let us not leave the sick alone! Let us not prevent them from finding consolation, or ourselves from being enriched by our closeness to those who suffer. Hospitals are true "cathedrals of suffering" where, however, the power of supportive and compassionate charity is also made evident.

—*General Audience, Saint Peter's Square, November 9, 2016*

DOCTOR OF SOULS AND BODIES

Jesus, on entering the house of Simon Peter, sees that his mother-in-law is in bed with a fever. He immediately takes her by the hand, heals her, and raises her. After sunset, since the Sabbath is over, the people can go out and bring the sick to him. He heals a multitude of people afflicted with maladies of every kind: physical, psychological, and spiritual. Having come to Earth to proclaim and to realize the salvation of the whole man and of all people, Jesus shows a particular predilection for those who are wounded in body and in spirit: the poor, the sinners, the possessed, the sick, the marginalized. Thus, he reveals himself as a doctor both of souls and of bodies, the Good Samaritan of man. He is the true Savior: Jesus saves, Jesus cures, Jesus heals.

—Angelus, *February 8, 2015*

THE SICK ARE ALWAYS WITH YOU

"The poor and the suffering you will always have with you," Jesus admonishes (cf. Mt 26:11), and the Church continually finds them along her path. She recognizes in those who are sick a privileged way to encounter Christ, to welcome and serve him. To treat the sick, to welcome them, to serve them, is to serve Christ: the sick are the flesh of Christ.

—Angelus, *February 8, 2015*

KINDNESS THERAPY

I bless you and the doctors bless you. All of you, dear children, receive a blessing each time you are cared for by the nurses, the staff, and everyone who works here. But you also have to learn how to bless them and to ask Jesus to look after them so that they can continue caring for you. Being here (and not only because of my age) I feel I can relate well with these two lessons of Simeon. On the one hand, entering here and seeing your eyes, your smiles—some impish—your faces, has filled me with a desire to give thanks. Thank you for the kind way that you welcomed me, thank you for recognizing the tenderness with which you are cared for here, the tenderness with which you are accompanied. Thank you for the efforts of many who are doing their best so that you can get better quickly.

It is very important that we feel cared for and accompanied, that we feel loved and that we know that all those who work here are looking for the best way to care for us. To each of these people, I say, "Thank you." "Thank you."

And at the same time, I wish to bless you. I ask God to bless you, and to accompany you and your families and all those people who work in this home and try to ensure that your smiles grow day by day. May God bless each person … not only the doctors but also those who provide "kindness therapy," thus making the time spent here more enjoyable. This "kindness therapy" is so important! So essential! Sometimes a caress can greatly help the process of healing.

Have you ever heard of the Indian Juan Diego? Or not? [The children respond: "Yes!"] Let's see now, all those who know him, raise your hands. When his uncle was sick, he was quite worried and distressed. Then, the Virgin of Guadalupe appeared to him and said, "Let not your heart be disturbed or upset by anything. Am I not here with you, I who am your mother?"

We have Mary as our Mother, and so let us ask her to give us the gift of her son, Jesus. And now, I want to ask all you children one thing: let's close our eyes, close them, and ask her to give us what our hearts seek today. Let us close our eyes and be still for a moment, and let us ask her what comes from our hearts.

—Visit to the Federico Gómez Pediatric Hospital, Mexico City,
February 14, 2016

THE SICK ONE IS JESUS

Saint Pio envisioned an extraordinary *corporal work of mercy*: the "Casa Sollievo della Sofferenza," inaugurated sixty years ago. He wanted it to be not just an excellent hospital, but a "temple of science and of prayer." Indeed, "human beings always need something more than technically proper care. They need humanity. They need heartfelt concern" (Benedict XVI, *Deus Caritas Est*, n. 31). This is so important: *to treat* the disease, but above all *to care* for those who are ill. Both are important, but they are two different things: treat the disease and the one who is sick. It can happen that, while the wounds of the body are treated, the wounds of the soul may worsen, and these are slower to detect and often difficult to heal. Even the dying, sometimes seemingly unconscious, take part in the prayer offered with faith by their side as they entrust themselves to God, to his mercy.

I remember the death of a priest friend. He was an apostle, a man of God. But he had been in a coma for a long time, a long time... The doctors were saying: "We don't know how he is still managing to breathe." Another priest friend came in, approached him, and spoke to him. He heard this priest's words: "Let the Lord take you. Let yourself go forward. Have faith, trust in the Lord." And with these words, he let himself go in peace.

So many people are in need, so many sick people, may they be spoken to, may they be caressed, may they be given the strength to bear their illness or go to meet the Lord. They need to be helped to entrust themselves to the Lord. I am so grateful to you and to those who serve the sick with competence, love, and faith. Let us ask for the grace to recognize the presence of Christ in those who are sick and suffering. As Padre Pio said again and again, "The sick person *is* Jesus." The sick one is Jesus. He or she is the flesh of Christ.

—*Address to Padre Pio Prayer Group, Saint Peter's Square,*
February 6, 2016

Bearing the Light

Each one of us is called to bear the light of the Word of God and the power of grace to those who suffer, and to those who assist them—family, doctors, nurses—so that service to the sick might always be better accomplished, with more humanity, with generous dedication, with evangelical love, with tenderness. Mother Church, through our hands, caresses our sufferings and treats our wounds, and does so with the tenderness of a mother.

—*Angelus, February 8, 2015*

A Gesture of Tenderness

In today's gospel (cf. Mk 1:40–45)...Jesus confronts an emblematic case, because the sick man is a leper. Leprosy is a contagious and pitiless disease that disfigures the person, and it was a symbol of impurity: a leper had to stay outside of inhabited areas and make his presence known to passersby. He was marginalized by the civil and religious community. He was like a dead man walking.

The episode of the healing of the leper takes place in three brief phases: the sick man's supplication, Jesus' response, and the consequences of the miraculous healing. The leper beseeches Jesus, "kneeling," and says to him: "If you will, you can make me clean" (v. 40). Jesus responds to this humble and trusting prayer because his soul is moved to deep pity: *compassion*. "Compassion" is a most profound word: compassion means "to suffer-with another." Jesus' heart manifests God's paternal compassion for that man, moving close to him and *touching him*. And this detail is very important. Jesus "stretched out his hand and *touched him*...And immediately the leprosy left him, and he was made clean" (vv. 41–42). God's mercy overcomes every barrier and Jesus' hand touches the leper. Jesus does not stand at a safe distance and does not act by delegating; he places himself in direct contact with our contagion. And thus our ills become the place of direct contact between us: He, Jesus, takes from us our diseased humanity and we take from him his sound and healing humanity. This happens each time we receive a sacrament with faith. The Lord Jesus "touches" us and grants us his grace. In this case we think especially of the sacrament of reconciliation, which heals us from the leprosy of sin.

Once again the Gospel shows us what God does in the face of our ills: God does not come to "give a lesson" on pain. Neither does he come to eliminate suffering and death from the world. Rather, he comes to take upon himself the burden of our human condition and carries it to the end, to free us in a radical and definitive way. This is how Christ fights the world's maladies and suffering: by taking them upon himself and conquering them with the power of God's mercy.

The gospel story of the healing of the leper tells us today that, if we want to be true disciples of Jesus, we are called to become, united to him, instruments of his merciful love, overcoming every kind of marginalization. In order to be "imitators of Christ" (cf. 1 Cor 11:1) in the face of a poor or sick person, we must not be afraid to look him in the eye and to draw near with tenderness and compassion, to touch him and embrace him. I have often asked this of people who help others, to do so looking them in the eye, to not to be afraid to touch them. This gesture of help may also be a gesture of communication: we too need to be welcomed by them. A gesture of tenderness, a gesture of compassion...

When you help others, do you look them in the eye? Do you embrace them without being afraid to touch them? Do you embrace them with tenderness? Think about this: How do you help? From a distance? Or with tenderness, with closeness? If evil is contagious, so is goodness. Therefore, there needs to be ever more abundant goodness in us. Let us be infected by goodness and let us spread goodness!

—Angelus, *February 15, 2015*

I too Am Spiritually Ill

It isn't easy to reach out to a sick person. Life's most beautiful things and most miserable things are modest, are hidden. Out of modesty, one tries to hide the greatest love; and out of modesty, we also seek to hide the things that show our human misery. This is why, when visiting a sick person, it is necessary to go to him or her, because the modesty of life hides them. Visit the sick. And when there are lifelong illnesses, when we have diseases that mark an entire life, we prefer to hide them, because to visit a sick person means visiting our own illness, that which we have inside. It is having the courage to say to oneself: I too have some disease in my heart, in my soul, in my spirit, I too am spiritually ill.

God created us to change the world, to be effective, to rule over creation: it is our task. But when we are confronted with disease, we see that illness prevents this: that man, that woman who was born that way, or whose body has become that way, it is like saying no—seemingly—to the mission of transforming the world. This is the mystery of sickness. One can approach illness only in the spirit of faith. We can draw near to a sick man, woman, boy, or girl, only if we look to him who took all of our sickness upon himself, if we become accustomed to looking at Christ crucified. The only explanation for this "failure," this human failure, a lifetime of sickness, is there. The only explanation is in Christ crucified.

I say to you, sick people, that if you cannot understand the Lord, I ask the Lord to enable you to understand in your heart that you are the flesh of Christ, that you are Christ crucified among us, that you are the brothers and sisters closest to Christ. It is one thing to look at a crucifix and it is another thing to look at a man, woman, child who is sick, in other words, crucified there in their illness: they are the living flesh of Christ.

Thanks so much to you volunteers! Thank you so much for spending your time caressing the flesh of Christ, serving the living Christ crucified. Thank you! And I also say thank you to you doctors and nurses. Thank you for doing this work, thank you for not making your profession a business... I ask all of you Christians of the diocese of Naples not to forget what Jesus asked of us and what is also written in the "protocol" on which we will be judged: I was sick and you visited me (cf. Mt 25:36). We will be judged on this. The world of illness is a world of pain. Sick people suffer, they reflect the suffering Christ: there is no need to fear drawing near to Christ who is suffering. Thank you so much for all that you do. Let us pray that all Christians of the diocese may have more awareness of this, and let us pray that the Lord may give perseverance to you and to so many volunteers in this service of caressing the suffering flesh of Christ. Thank you.

—Visit with the sick in the Basilica of Gesù Nuovo, Naples,
March 21, 2015

BLOOD DONORS

Dear brothers and sisters, today is World Blood Donor Day. Millions of people contribute, in a silent way, to aid our brothers and sisters in difficulty. To all donors, I express appreciation and I invite especially young people to follow their example.

—Angelus, June 14, 2015

Visiting the Prisoner

LET NO ONE POINT A FINGER

I think of those who are locked up in prison. Jesus has not forgotten them either. By including the act of visiting of those in prison among the works of mercy, he wanted first and foremost to invite us to judge no one. Of course, if someone is in prison it is because he has done wrong, and did not respect the law or civil harmony. Therefore, in prison, he is serving his sentence. However, whatever a detainee may have done, he remains always loved by God.

Who is able to enter the depths of [an inmate's] conscience to understand what he is experiencing? Who can understand his suffering and remorse? It is too easy to wash our hands, declaring that he has done wrong. A Christian is called, above all, to assume responsibility, so that whoever has done wrong understands the evil he has carried out and returns to his senses. The absence of freedom is, without a doubt, one of the hardest pills for a human being to swallow. Add this to the degradation arising from the conditions, often devoid of humanity, in which such persons live, then it truly becomes a situation in which a Christian is challenged to do everything possible to restore their dignity.

Visiting people in prison is a work of mercy that, especially today, takes on a particular value due to the various forms of "Peronista justice" to which we are exposed. Therefore, let no one point a finger at another. Instead, let us all be instruments of mercy and have attitudes of sharing and respect.

I often think about detainees...I think of them often, I carry them in my heart. I wonder what led them to delinquency, and how they managed to succumb to various forms of evil. Yet, along with these thoughts, I feel that they all need closeness and tenderness, because God's mercy works wonders. How many tears I have seen on the cheeks of prisoners who had perhaps never wept before in their lives, and who now weep only because they feel welcomed and loved.

—General Audience, Saint Peter's Square, November 9, 2016

TRUE FREEDOM

Hope is a gift of God. We must ask for it. It is placed deep within each human heart in order to shed light on this life, so often troubled and clouded by so many situations that bring sadness and pain. We need to nourish the roots of our hope so that they can bear fruit; primarily, the certainty of God's closeness and compassion despite whatever evil we have done. There is no corner of our heart that cannot be touched by God's love. Whenever someone makes a mistake, the Father's mercy is all the more present, awakening repentance, forgiveness, reconciliation, and peace.

Today we celebrate the Jubilee of Mercy for you and with you, our brothers and sisters who are imprisoned. Mercy, as the expression of God's love, is something we need to think about more deeply. Certainly, breaking the law involves paying a price, and losing one's freedom is the worst part of serving time, because it affects us so deeply. All the same, hope must not falter. Paying for the wrong we have done is one thing, but another thing entirely is the "breath" of hope, which cannot be stifled by anyone or anything. Our heart always yearns for goodness. We are in debt to the mercy that God constantly shows us, for he never abandons us (cf. Augustine, *Sermo* 254:1)...

Dear friends, today is your Jubilee! Today, in God's sight, may your hope be kindled anew. A jubilee, by its very nature, always brings with it a proclamation of freedom (Lev 25:39–46). It does not depend on me to grant this, but the Church's duty, one she cannot renounce, is to awaken within you the desire for *true* freedom. Sometimes, a certain hypocrisy leads people to consider you only as wrongdoers, for whom prison is the sole answer. I want to tell you that every time I visit a prison, I ask myself: "Why them and not me?" We can all make mistakes: all of us. And in one way or another we have made mistakes. Hypocrisy leads us to overlook the possibility that people can change their lives. We put little trust in rehabilitation, rehabilitation into society. But in this way we forget that we are all sinners, and often, without being aware of it, we too are prisoners. At times we are locked up within our own prejudices or enslaved to the idols of a false sense of wellbeing. At times we get stuck in our own ideologies or absolutize the laws of the market even as they crush other people. At such times, we imprison ourselves behind the walls of individualism and self-sufficiency, deprived of the truth that sets us free. Pointing the finger at someone who has made mistakes cannot become an alibi for concealing our own contradictions.

—*Homily, Jubilee for Prisoners, November 6, 2016*

No Worse than You and Me

Mother Church teaches us to be close to those who are in prison. "But no, Father, this is dangerous, those are bad people." But each of us is capable . . . Listen carefully to this: each of us is capable of doing the same thing that that man or that woman in prison did. All of us have the capacity to sin and to do the same, to make mistakes in life. They are no worse than you and me! Mercy overcomes every wall, every barrier, and leads you to always seek the human face, of the the face of the person. And it is mercy that changes the heart and the life, that can regenerate a person and allow him or her to integrate into society in a new way.

—*General Audience, Saint Peter's Square, September 10, 2014*

The Encounter with God

A true and complete reintegration of the person does not come about as the end of an exclusively human journey. This path also involves *an encounter with God*, the ability to allow ourselves to be looked at by God, who loves us. It is more difficult to allow God to look at us than it is to look at God. It is more difficult to allow God to encounter us than to encounter God, because we always resist. He waits for us, he looks at us, he always seeks us, this God who loves us, who is capable of understanding us and forgiving our mistakes. The Lord is a master at reintegrating people. He takes us by the hand and brings us back to society and the community. The Lord always forgives, always accompanies, and always understands. It is up to us to allow ourselves to be understood, to be forgiven, and to be accompanied.

—Visit to the penitentiary in Castrovillari, June 21, 2014

Reintegration

This is the challenge, as I was saying two weeks ago at the prison of Castrovillari: the challenge is social reintegration. And for this, you need an itinerary, a route, whether outside, in the prison, in society, or whether inside oneself, in the conscience and in the heart.

To make the journey of reintegration: this is something all of us must do. Everyone. All of us make mistakes in life. And all of us must ask forgiveness for these mistakes and undertake the journey of reintegration, in order not to make such mistakes any more. Some make this journey at home, in their own work; others, like you, in a penitentiary. But everyone, everyone must make it...Whoever says he does not need to make a journey of reintegration is a liar! All of us make mistakes in life and all of us, too, are sinners. And when we go to ask the Lord for forgiveness for our sins, for our mistakes, he always forgives us. He never tires of forgiving. He tells us: "Turn your back on this path, this is not the right one for you." And he helps us. And this is reintegration, the journey that we all have to make.

What is important is not to stand still. We all know that when water stands still it stagnates. Do not stand still. We all have to walk, to take a step every day, with the Lord's help. God is Father, he is mercy, he always loves us. If we seek him, he welcomes us and forgives us. As I said, he never tires of forgiving. This is the motto of this visit: "God doesn't tire of forgiving." He makes us rise and fully restores our dignity. God has a memory, he is not forgetful. God does not forget us, he always remembers. There is a passage in the Bible, from the prophet Isaiah, which says: "Even should a mother forget her child"—which is impossible—"I will never forget you" (cf. Is 49:15). And this is true: God thinks about me, God remembers me. I am in God's memory.

And with this trust, we can walk, day by day. And with this steadfast love that accompanies us, hope will not let us down. With this love hope will never let us down: a steadfast love to go forward with the Lord . . . I'll tell you something personal. When I meet with one of you who is in jail, who is moving toward reintegration, but who is imprisoned, I sincerely wonder: Why him and not me? I feel this way. It's a mystery. But beginning with this feeling, with this feeling I accompany you.

—Visit with prisoners in the penitentiary in Isernia, July 5, 2014

JESUS IS A PRISONER

I thank you and I would like to take advantage of this meeting with you, who work in the prisons throughout

Italy, to send my greetings to all the inmates. Please tell them that I am praying for them, I have them in my heart, I am praying to the Lord and to Our Lady that they may be able to get through this difficult period in their lives in a positive way, that they may not become discouraged or closed in on themselves. You know how one day things go well, but the next day they feel discouraged, and this fluctuation is difficult. The Lord is close, but tell them with your actions, with your words, and with your hearts that the Lord does not remain outside. He does not remain outside their cells, he does not remain outside the prison; rather, he is inside, he is there. You can say this: the Lord is inside with them; he too is a prisoner. Even today, he is imprisoned by our egoism, by our systems, by so many injustices, for it is easy to punish the weakest while the big fish swim freely in the sea. No cell is so isolated that it is shut to the Lord, none. He is there, he weeps with them, he works with them, he hopes with them, his paternal and maternal love reaches everywhere. I pray that each one may open his heart to this love. When I would receive a letter from one of the inmates in Buenos Aires I would visit him. Now when those from Buenos Aires write to me I sometimes phone them for a chat, especially on Sunday. When I finish, I think: Why is he there and not I who have so many and different reasons to be there? Thinking about this does me good. Seeing that we share the same weaknesses, I ask: Why did he fall and I did not? This is a mystery that makes me pray and makes me draw close to inmates.

I also pray for you who are chaplains and for your ministry, which is difficult. It is very demanding and very important, since it expresses one of the works of mercy: to

make the Lord's presence visible in the prison, in the prison cell. You are a sign of the closeness of Christ to these brothers who are in need of hope. Recently you spoke about a justice of reconciliation, but also about a justice of hope, open doors, and horizons. This is not a utopia, it can be done. It is not easy, for our weaknesses are everywhere, the devil is also everywhere, and temptations are everywhere; but we must always try.

It is my sincere wish that the Lord be always with you, that he bless you, and that Our Lady watch over you. Let yourselves remain always in the hands of Our Lady, for she is the mother of you and of all those in prison. This is my wish for you, thank you! And let us ask the Lord to bless you and all of your friends in the prisons. But let us first pray to Our Lady that she may always lead us to Jesus: *Hail Mary* . . .

—Address to a national conference of prison chaplains, the Vatican,
October 23, 2013

LOVE THAT TRANFORMS

Dear brothers, I know of your painful situations; I receive many letters—some extremely moving—from prisons all over the world. Inmates are often held in conditions unworthy of the human condition, and then they are not able to reintegrate into society. But thanks be to God there are also directors, chaplains, educators, and pastoral workers who know how to be close to you in the right way. There are several good and meaningful experiences of reintegration. Work on this, develop these positive experiences that allow a different attitude to be cultivated in the civil community

and in the Church community. The basis of this commitment is the conviction that love is always able to transform the human person. Thus a place of marginalization—such as, in a negative sense, a prison—can become a place of inclusion and a stimulus for the whole of society, so that it may be more just and attentive to the people.

I invite you to live each day and each moment in the presence of God, to whom the future of the world and humankind belongs. This is Christian hope: the future is in God's hands! History makes sense because it dwells in God's goodness.

Therefore, even in the midst of so many problems— even serious ones—we cannot lose our hope in God's infinite mercy and his providence. With this certain hope, let us prepare ourselves for Easter, which is now approaching, decisively directing our lives to the Lord and keeping the flame of his love alive in us.

—Visit with prisoners at the Giuseppe Salvia Detention Center, Naples, March 21, 2015

SAVED FROM MANY SINS

You may be asking yourselves: "Who is this man standing before us?" I would like to reply to that question with something absolutely certain in my own life. The man standing before you is a man who has experienced forgiveness. A man who was, and is, saved from his many sins. That is who I am. I don't have much more to give you or to offer you, but I want to share with you what I do have and what I love. It is Jesus Christ, the mercy of the Father.

Jesus came to show the love that God has for us. For you, for each of you, and for me. It is a love that is powerful and real. It is a love that takes seriously the plight of those he loves. It is a love that heals, forgives, raises up, and shows concern. It is a love that draws near and restores dignity. We can lose this dignity in so many ways. But Jesus is stubborn; he gave his very life in order to restore the identity we had lost, to clothe us with the power of his dignity.

Here is something that can help us understand this. Peter and Paul, disciples of Jesus, were also prisoners. They too lost their freedom. But there was something that sustained them, something that did not let them yield to despair, that did not let them sink into darkness and meaninglessness. That something was prayer. It was prayer, both individual and with others. They prayed, and they prayed for one another. These two forms of prayer became a network to maintain life and hope. And that network keeps us from yielding to despair. It encourages us to keep moving forward. It is a network that supports life, your own lives and those of your families.

When Jesus becomes part of our lives, we can no longer remain imprisoned by our past. Instead, we begin to look to the present, and we see it differently, with a different kind of hope. We begin to see ourselves and our lives in a different light. We are no longer stuck in the past, but become capable of shedding tears and finding in them the strength to make a new start. If there are times when we experience sadness, when we're in a bad way, when we're depressed or have negative feelings, I ask that we look at Christ crucified. Look at his face; in his eyes there is a place for us. We can all bring to Christ our wounds, our pain, our mistakes, our sins, and all those things that perhaps we got wrong. In the wounds of Jesus, there is a place for our own wounds. We are all wounded, in one way or another. And so we bring our wounds to the wounds of Jesus. Why? So that there they can be soothed, washed clean, transformed, and healed. He died for you, for me, so that he could stretch out his hand and lift us up. Speak to the priests who come here, talk to them! Speak to the brothers and sisters who come, speak to them. Speak to everyone who comes here to talk to you about Jesus. Jesus wants to help you get up, always.

— *Visit to the Re-education Center of Santa Cruz de la Sierra, Bolivia,*
July 10, 2015

THE LORD WHO WASHES OUR FEET

Thank you for receiving me and giving me the opportunity to be here with you and to share this time in your lives. It is a difficult time, one full of struggles. I know it is a painful time, not only for you but also for your families and for all of society. Any society, any family, that cannot share or take seriously the pain of its children and views that pain as something normal or to be expected is a society "condemned" to remain a hostage to itself, prey to the very things which cause that pain.

I am here as a pastor, but above all as a brother, to share your situation and to make it my own. I have come so that we can pray together and offer our God everything that causes us pain, but also everything that gives us hope, so that we can receive from him the power of the resurrection.

I think of the gospel scene where Jesus washes the feet of his disciples at the Last Supper. This was something his disciples found hard to accept. Even Peter refused, and told him: "You will never wash my feet" (Jn 13:8).

In those days, it was the custom to wash someone's feet when they came to your home. That was how they welcomed people. The roads were not paved, they were covered with dust, and little stones would get stuck in your sandals. Everyone walked those roads, which left their feet dusty, bruised, or cut from the stones. That is why we see Jesus washing feet, our feet, the feet of his disciples, then and now.

We all know that life is a journey, along different roads, different paths that leave their mark on us.

We also know in faith that Jesus seeks us out. He wants to heal our wounds, to soothe our feet that hurt from travelling alone, to wash each of us clean of the dust from our journey. He doesn't ask us where we have been, he doesn't question us about what we have done. Rather, he tells us: "Unless I wash your feet, you have no share with me" (Jn 13:8). Unless I wash your feet, I will not be able to give you the life that the Father always dreamed of, the life for which he created you. Jesus comes to meet us so that he can restore our dignity as children of God. He wants to help us to set out again, to resume our journey, to recover our hope, to restore our faith and trust. He wants us to keep walking along the paths of life, to realize that we have a mission, and that confinement is never the same thing as exclusion.

Life means "getting our feet dirty" from the dust-filled roads of life and history. All of us need to be cleansed, to be washed. All of us. Myself, first and foremost. All of us are being sought out by the Teacher, who wants to help us resume our journey. The Lord goes in search of us; to all of us he stretches out a helping hand.

It is painful when we see prison systems that are not concerned with caring for wounds, with soothing pain, with offering new possibilities. It is painful when we see people who think that only others need to be cleansed or purified and do not recognize that their weariness, pain, and wounds are also the weariness, pain, and wounds of society. The Lord tells us this clearly with a sign: he washes our feet so we can come back to the table, the table from which he wishes no one to be excluded, the table that is spread for all and to which all of us are invited.

This time in your life can have only one purpose: to give you a hand in getting back on the right road, to give you a hand to help you rejoin society. All of us are part of that effort, all of us are invited to encourage, help, and enable your rehabilitation, a rehabilitation that everyone—inmates and their families, correctional authorities, those working in social and educational programs—seeks and desires, a rehabilitation that benefits and elevates the morale of the entire community and society.

I encourage you to have this attitude with one another and with all those who in any way are part of this institution. May you make possible new opportunities; may you blaze new trails, new paths.

All of us have something we need to be cleansed of or purified from. All of us. May the knowledge of this fact inspire us all to live in solidarity, to support one another and seek the best for others.

Let us look to Jesus, who washes our feet. He is "the way, and the truth, and the life." He comes to save us from the lie that says no one can change, the lie of thinking that no one can change. Jesus helps us to journey along the paths of life and fulfillment. May the power of his love and his resurrection always lead you to new life.

—Visit with detainees in the Curran-Fromhold Correctional Institute, Philadelphia, September 27, 2015

THINGS CAN CHANGE

Divine Mercy reminds us that prisons are an indication of the kind of society we live in. In many cases they are a sign of the silence and omissions that have led to a throwaway culture, a symptom of a culture that has stopped supporting life, of a society that has little by little abandoned its children.

Mercy reminds us that reintegration does not begin here within these walls; rather, it begins before, it begins "outside," in the streets of the city. Reintegration or rehabilitation begins by creating a system that we could call social health, that is, a society that seeks not to cause sickness, polluting relationships in neighborhoods, schools, town squares, the streets, homes, and across the whole of the social spectrum. A system of social health endeavors to promote a culture that is effective, one that seeks to prevent such situations, which end up damaging and impairing the social fabric.

At times it may seem that prisons are intended more to prevent people from committing crimes than to promote the process of reintegration that allows us to address the social, psychological, and family problems that lead a person to act in a certain way. The problem of security is not resolved only by incarceration. Rather, it calls us to intervene by confronting the structural and cultural causes of insecurity that impact the entire social framework.

Jesus' concern for the care of the hungry, the thirsty, the homeless, and prisoners (cf. Mt 25:34–40) sought to express the core of the Father's mercy. This becomes a moral imperative for the whole of a society that wishes to maintain the necessary conditions for a better common life. A society's capacity to include the poor, infirm, and imprisoned makes it possible for them to be healed of their wounds and begin sharing in the work of building a peaceful community. Social reintegration begins by making sure that all of our children go to school and that their families obtain dignified work; by creating public spaces for leisure and recreation; and by fostering civic participation, health services, and access to basic services, to name just a few possible measures. This is where every process of reintegration begins.

Celebrating the Jubilee of Mercy with you means learning not to be prisoners of the past, of yesterday. It means learning to open the door to the future, to tomorrow. It means believing that things can change. Celebrating the Jubilee of Mercy with you means inviting you to lift up your heads and to work in order to gain this space of longed-for freedom. Celebrating the Jubilee of Mercy with you means repeating that phrase that we just heard, put so well and so clearly: "When they sentenced me, someone said: 'Don't ask why you are here but for what purpose.'" And this "for what purpose" must carry us forward, this "for what purpose" must help us overcome the barrier of the social illusion that makes people believe that safety and order can be achieved only by incarcerating people.

We know that we cannot turn back, we know that what is done is done. But I wanted to celebrate the Jubilee of Mercy with you, so that it may be clear that it does not exclude the possibility of writing a new story, a new story that moves into the future: the "for what purpose." You suffer the pain of a failure—if only we could all suffer the discomfort of our concealed and cloaked failures—you feel the remorse of your actions and, in many cases, with great limitations you seek to remake your lives in the midst of solitude. You have known the power of sorrow and sin, and have not forgotten that within your reach is the power of the resurrection, the power of divine mercy that makes all things new. Now you face the part that is hardest and most difficult, and yet perhaps it is this part that can bear the greatest fruit. From inside this prison, you must work hard to change the situations that create the most exclusion. Speak with your loved ones, tell them of your experiences, help them to put an end to this cycle of violence and exclusion. The one who has suffered the greatest pain, the one who, we could say, "has experienced hell," can become a prophet in society. Work so that this society that uses people and discards them will not go on claiming victims.

In saying this to you I recall what Jesus said: "Let him who has no sin cast the first stone"; I too would have to go away. In saying this to you, I do not do so like someone wagging his finger from on high; I do so from the experience of my own wounds, mistakes, and sins for which the Lord willed to pardon and correct me. I do so aware that without his grace and my vigilance I could repeat the same mistakes. Brothers and sisters, on entering a prison I always ask myself: "Why them and not me?" This is a mystery of divine mercy; and that divine mercy we are celebrating today, all of us looking ahead with hope.

I wish also to encourage those who work in this center or others like it: the directors, the prison guards, and all who undertake any type of work here. And I am also grateful for the efforts made by the chaplains, consecrated persons, and lay faithful who have dedicated themselves to keeping alive the hope of the Gospel of Mercy in the prison, by the pastors, by all who come here to give you the word of God. Never forget that all of you can be signs of the Father's heart. We need one another, as our sister has just said to us, recalling the Letter to the Hebrews: "Feel yourselves imprisoned for one another."

Before giving you my blessing, I would like us to pray in silence, all of us together. Each one knows what he wants to say to the Lord, each one knows what to ask forgiveness for. But I also ask that in this silent prayer we may open our hearts so that we can forgive a society that did not know how to help us and that so many times led us to make mistakes. From the depths of our hearts, may each one of us ask God to help us believe in his mercy. Let us pray in silence.

—*Visit to the penitentiary in Ciudad Juárez, Mexico,*
February 17, 2016

Burying the Dead

While conscious of the threat posed by a globalization of indifference, we should also recognize that ... there are also many positive initiatives that testify to the compassion, mercy, and solidarity of which we are capable.

Here I would offer some examples of praiseworthy commitment, which demonstrate how all of us can overcome indifference in choosing not to close our eyes to our neighbor. These represent good practices on the way to a more humane society.

There are many non-governmental and charitable organizations, both within and outside the Church, whose members, amid epidemics, disasters, and armed conflicts, brave difficulties and dangers in caring for the injured and the sick, and in burying the dead. I would also mention those individuals and associations that assist migrants who cross deserts and seas in search of a better life. These efforts are spiritual and corporal works of mercy on which we will be judged at the end of our lives.

—*Message for the World Day of Peace, January 1, 2016*

The Gate of Heaven

Mother Church teaches us to be close to those who are neglected and die alone. That is what the blessed Teresa did on the streets of Calcutta; that is what has been and is being done by many Christians who are not afraid to hold the hand of someone who is about to leave this world. And here too, mercy gives peace to those who pass away and those who remain, allowing them to feel that God is greater than death, and that abiding in him even the last parting is a "see you again"... The blessed Teresa understood this well! They told her: "Mother, this is a waste of time!" She found people dying on the street, people whose bodies were being eaten by rats on the street, and she took them home so they could die in cleanliness, calm, touched gently, in peace. She gave them a "see you again," all of them... And so many men and women like her have done this. And they are awaiting them, there [pointing to heaven], at the gate, to open the gate of Heaven to them. Help people die serenely, in peace.

—*General Audience, Saint Peter's Square, September 10, 2014*

God Never Abandons Us

Many of you have suffered greatly, not only from the destruction caused by the storm, but from the loss of family members and friends. Today let us commend to God's mercy all those who have died and invoke his consolation and peace upon all who still grieve. May we remember in a particular way those among us whose pain makes it hard for them to see the way forward. At the same time, let us thank the Lord for all those who have labored in these months to clear away the rubble, to visit the sick and the dying, to comfort the grieving, and to bury the dead. Their goodness, and the generous aid that came from so many people throughout the world, are a real sign that God never abandons us!

Meeting with priests, religious, and seminarians, and families of survivors,

—Cathedral of Palo, Philippines, January 17, 2015

An Act of Compassion and of Faith

The last corporal work of mercy calls us to *bury the dead*. This may seem a curious request, although, in certain regions of the world that are living under the scourge of war, with bombings day and night sowing fear and claiming innocent victims, sadly this work is timely. The Bible gives a fine example in this regard: that of the elderly Tobit, who, risking his life, would go out to bury the dead in spite of the king's prohibition (cf. Tob 1:17–19, 2:2–4). Today too, there are those who risk their lives to bury unfortunate victims of war. Thus, this corporal work of mercy is not far from our daily existence. It makes us ponder what happened on Good Friday, when the Virgin Mary, John, and several women were near Jesus' cross. After the death of Jesus, Joseph of Arimathea—a rich member of the Sanhedrin who had become a follower of Jesus—came and offered his own tomb, newly hewn out of the rock, for Jesus. He personally went to Pilate and asked for Jesus' body: a true work of mercy performed with great courage (cf. Mt 27:57–60)! For Christians, burial is an act of compassion, but also an act of great faith. We bury the bodies of our loved ones, in the hope of their resurrection (cf. 1 Cor 15:1–34). This is a rite that endures among and is meaningful for our people, and that has a special resonance in this month of November, which is dedicated in particular to prayer for the departed.

—General Audience, November 30, 2016

III

THE SPIRITUAL
WORKS OF MERCY

Counseling the Doubtful

An Offer

To those today who "wish to see Jesus," to those who are searching for the face of God; to those who received catechesis when they were little and then developed it no further and perhaps have lost their faith; to so many who have not yet encountered Jesus personally... to all these people we can offer three things: *the Gospel, the crucifix, and the witness of our faith,* poor but sincere. The Gospel: there we can encounter Jesus, listen to him, know him. The crucifix: the sign of the love of Jesus who gave himself for us. And then a faith that is expressed in simple gestures of fraternal charity. But mainly in the coherence of life, between what we say and what we do. Coherence between our faith and our life, between our words and our actions: Gospel, crucifix, witness.

—Angelus, *March 22, 2015*

A Dogmatic Certainty

I have a dogmatic certainty: God is in every person's life. God is in everyone's life. Even if the life of a person has been

113

a disaster, even if it is destroyed by vices, drugs, or anything else—God is in this person's life. You can, you must try to seek God in every human life. Although the life of a person is a land full of thorns and weeds, there is always a space in which the good seed can grow. You have to trust God.

— *"A Big Heart Open to God," Interview in* America,
September 30, 2013

CHALLENGES HELP US GROW

The joy of the Gospel is such that it cannot be taken away from us by anyone or anything (cf. Jn 16:22). The evils of our world—and those of the Church—must not be excuses for diminishing our commitment and our fervor. Let us look upon them as challenges that can help us to grow. With the eyes of faith, we can see the light which the Holy Spirit always radiates in the midst of darkness, never forgetting that "where sin increased, grace has abounded all the more" (Rom 5:20). Our faith is challenged to discern how wine can come from water and how wheat can grow in the midst of weeds. Fifty years after the Second Vatican Council, we are distressed by the troubles of our age and far from naive optimism; yet the fact that we are more realistic must not mean that we are any less trusting in the Spirit or less generous. In this sense, we can once again listen to the words of Blessed John XXIII, on the memorable day of October 11, 1962:

At times we have to listen, much to our regret, to the voices of people who, though burning with zeal, lack a sense of discretion and measure. In this modern age they can see nothing but prevarication and ruin... We feel that we must disagree with those prophets of doom who are always forecasting disaster, as though the end of the world were at hand. In our times, Divine Providence is leading us to a new order of human relations which, by human effort and even beyond all expectations, are directed to the fulfillment of God's superior and inscrutable designs, in which everything, even human setbacks, leads to the greater good of the Church.

—Evangelii Gaudium, *84*

UNCERTAINTY

In this quest to seek and find God in all things there is still an area of uncertainty. There must be. If a person says that he met God with total certainty and is not touched by a margin of uncertainty, then this is not good. For me, this is an important key. If one has the answers to all the questions—that is the proof that God is not with him. It means that he is a false prophet using religion for himself. The great leaders of the people of God, like Moses, have always left room for doubt. You must leave room for the Lord, not for our certainties; we must be humble. Uncertainty is in every true discernment that is open to finding confirmation in spiritual consolation...

All of our ancestors in the faith died seeing the good that was promised, but from a distance... Our life is not given to us like an opera libretto, in which all is written down; but it means going, walking, doing, searching, seeing... We must enter into the adventure of the quest for meeting God; we must let God search and encounter us.

— *"A Big Heart Open to God,"* Interview in America,
September 30, 2013

SPIRITUAL DESERTIFICATION

One of the more serious temptations that stifle boldness and zeal is a defeatism that turns us into querulous and disillusioned pessimists, "sourpusses." Nobody can go off to battle unless he is fully convinced of victory beforehand. If we start without confidence, we have already lost half the battle and we bury our talents. While painfully aware of our own frailties, we have to march on without giving in, keeping in mind what the Lord said to Saint Paul: "My grace is sufficient for you, for my power is made perfect in weakness" (2 Cor 12:9). Christian triumph is always a cross, yet a cross which is at the same time a victorious banner borne with aggressive tenderness against the assaults of evil. The evil spirit of defeatism is brother to the temptation to separate, before its time, the wheat from the weeds; it is the fruit of an anxious and self-centered lack of trust.

In some places a spiritual "desertification" has evidently come about... Yet "it is starting from the experience of this desert, from this void, that we can again discover the joy of believing, its vital importance for us men and women. In the desert we rediscover the value of what is essential for living; thus in today's world there are innumerable signs, often expressed implicitly or negatively, of the thirst for God, for the ultimate meaning of life. And in the desert people of faith are needed who, by the example of their own lives, point out the way to the Promised Land and keep hope alive" (Pope Benedict XVI). In these situations we are called to be living sources of water from which others can drink. At times, this becomes a heavy cross, but it was from the cross, from his pierced side, that our Lord gave himself to us as a source of living water. Let us not allow ourselves to be robbed of hope!

—Evangelii Gaudium, *85–86*

SIGNS OF THE RESURRECTION

Christ's resurrection is not an event of the past; it contains a vital power that has permeated this world. Where all seems to be dead, signs of the resurrection suddenly spring up. It is an irresistible force. Often it seems that God does not exist: all around us we see persistent injustice, evil, indifference, and cruelty. But it is also true that in the midst of darkness something new always springs to life and sooner or later produces fruit. On razed land life breaks through, stubbornly and invincibly. However dark things are, goodness always re-emerges and spreads. Each day in our world beauty is born anew; it rises transformed through the storms of history. Values always tend to reappear under new guises, and human beings have arisen time after time from situations that seemed doomed. Such is the power of the resurrection, and all who evangelize are instruments of that power.

—Evangelii Gaudium, *276*

GOD IS IN EVERY SITUATION

The kingdom is here, it returns, it struggles to flourish anew. Christ's resurrection everywhere calls forth seeds of that new world; even if they are cut back, they grow again, for the resurrection is already secretly woven into the fabric of this history, for Jesus did not rise in vain. May we never remain on the sidelines of this march of living hope!

Because we do not always see these seeds growing, we need an interior certainty, a conviction that God is able to act in every situation, even amid apparent setbacks...It involves knowing with certitude that all those who entrust themselves to God in love will bear good fruit (cf. Jn 15:5). This fruitfulness is often invisible, elusive, and unquantifiable. We can know quite well that our lives will be fruitful, without claiming to know how, or where, or when. We may be sure that none of our acts of love will be lost, nor any of our acts of sincere concern for others. No single act of love for God will be lost, no generous effort is meaningless, no painful endurance is wasted. All of these encircle our world like a vital force. Sometimes it seems that our work is fruitless, but mission is not like a business transaction or investment, or even a humanitarian activity. It is not a show where we count how many people come as a result of our publicity; it is something much deeper, which escapes all measurement. It may be that the Lord uses our sacrifices to shower blessings in another part of the world that we will never visit. The Holy Spirit works as he wills, when he wills, and where he wills; we entrust ourselves without pretending to see striking results. We know only that our commitment is necessary. Let us learn to rest in the tenderness of the arms of the Father amid our creative and generous commitment. Let us keep marching forward; let us give him everything, allowing him to make our efforts bear fruit in his good time.

—Evangelii Gaudium, *278–79*

DOUBTS THAT BRING GROWTH

A good education teaches us the critical method, which also includes a certain kind of doubt, the kind used for asking questions and verifying the answers, with a view to greater knowledge. However, the work of mercy of counseling the doubtful is not about this kind of doubt. Rather, it is about expressing mercy toward those who doubt, alleviating that pain and suffering that come from the fear and anguish caused by doubt. It is therefore an act of true love, whereby support is given to someone in a state of weakness caused by uncertainty.

I think some of you might ask me: "Father, but I have many doubts about the faith; what should I do? Don't you ever have doubts?" I have many... Of course, everyone has doubts at times! Doubts that touch the faith, in a positive way, are a sign that we want to know better and more fully God, Jesus, and the mystery of his love for us. "Still, I have this doubt: I seek, I study, I consult, or I ask advice about what to do." These are doubts that bring about growth! It is good, therefore, that we ask questions about our faith, because in this way we are pushed to deepen it. Doubts, however, must also be overcome. For this, it is necessary to listen to the Word of God, and to understand what he teaches us. An important help to doing this is *catechesis*, in which the proclamation of the faith is encountered in the concreteness of individual and community life. And there is, at the same time, another equally important help, that of *living* the faith as much as possible. Let us not make of faith an abstract theory where doubts multiply. Rather, let us make of faith our life. Let us seek to practice it in service to our brothers and sisters, especially those who are most in need. And thus, many doubts disappear, because we feel the presence of God and the truth of the Gospel in love, which—without our deserving it—lives in us, and we share it with others...

The most profound lesson that we are called to transmit, and the most certain way to free ourselves of doubt, is the love of God with which we have been loved (cf. 1 Jn 4:10): a great love, free, and given to us forever. God never goes back on his love! He always moves forward and waits. He forever gives us love, to which we must feel the steadfast responsibility of being witnesses by offering mercy to our brothers and sisters.

—General Audience, November 23, 2016

Instructing the Ignorant

Every family needs a father. Today we shall reflect on the value of his role, and I would like to begin with a passage that we find in the Book of Proverbs, words that a father addresses to his own son. It reads like this: "My son, if your heart is wise, my heart too will be glad. My soul will rejoice when your lips speak what is right" (Pr 23:15–16). Nothing could better express the pride and emotion a father feels when he understands that he has handed down to his child what really matters in life, that is, a wise heart. This father does not say: "I am proud of you because you are the same as me, because you repeat the things I say and do." No, he does not say anything so simple to him. He says something much more important, which we can understand in this way: "I will be happy every time I see you act with wisdom, and I will be moved every time that I hear you speak with rectitude. This is what I wanted to leave to you, that this one thing become yours: the attitude to feel and act, to speak and judge with wisdom and rectitude. And that you might be like this, I taught you the things you didn't know, I corrected the errors you didn't see. I made you feel a profound and at the same time discreet affection, which maybe you did not fully recognize when you were young and unsure. I gave you a testimony of rigor and steadfastness that perhaps you didn't understand, when you would have liked only complicity and protection. I first had to test myself in terms of the wisdom of my own heart, and I had to be vigilant with regard to excesses of sentiment and resentment in order to bear the weight of the inevitable misunderstandings and to find the right words to make myself understood. Now," continues the father, "I see that you strive to be this way with your own children, and with everyone, and it moves me. I am happy to be your father." This is what a wise father, a mature father, says.

—*General Audience, Saint Peter's Square, February 4, 2015*

FAMILY EDUCATION

Today we will pause to reflect on an essential characteristic of the family, the natural vocation to *educate children* so they may grow up to be responsible for themselves and for others. What we heard from the apostle Paul...is very beautiful: "Children, obey your parents in everything, for this pleases the Lord. Fathers, do not provoke your children, lest they become discouraged" (Col 3:20–21). This is a wise rule: children should be raised to listen to their parents and obey their parents, who, in turn, should not order them around in a negative way, so as not to discourage the children. Children, indeed, must grow without becoming discouraged, step by step.

If you parents say to your children: "Let's climb this ladder" and you take them by the hand and, step by step, help them climb, things will go well. But if you say: "Go up!"— "But I can't"—"Go!", this is called provoking your children, asking them to do things they don't have the ability to do. That is why the relationship between parents and children must be one of wisdom, of a great balance. Children, obey your parents, this pleases God. And you parents, don't provoke your children by asking of them things they can't do. And this needs to be done so that children can grow up to be responsible for themselves and for others.

This would seem quite obvious, but there is no shortage of difficulties in our times. It is hard to educate when parents see their children only in the evening, when they come home tired from work. Well, those who are fortunate enough to work! It is even more difficult for parents who are separated, who are weighed down by their condition: poor people, they have real hardships. They are separated, and frequently the child is taken hostage, and the father speaks ill of the mother, and the mother speaks ill of the father, and so much harm is done.

But I say to separated parents: never, never, never take your child hostage! You separated because of many difficulties and reasons. Life has given you this trial, but the children should not be the ones to carry the weight of the separation, they should not be used as hostages against the other spouse, they should grow up hearing their mother speak well of their father, even though the parents are not together, and the father speak well of their mother. For separated parents this is very important and very difficult, but they can do it.

Above all, the question is: how should we educate? What tradition do we have today to pass on to our children?

Intellectual "critics" of every kind have silenced parents in countless ways, in order to protect the younger generations from the damage—real or presumed—of family education. The family stands accused, among other things, of being authoritarian, of favoritism, of conformism, of the emotional repression that generates conflict.

In fact, a rift has opened up between the family and society, between the family and school. The educational pact today has been broken, and thus the educational alliance between society and the family is in crisis because mutual trust has been undermined. There are many symptoms. For example, at school relationships between parents and teachers have been compromised. Sometimes there is tension and mutual distrust, and naturally the consequences are felt by the children. On the other hand, the number of so-called "experts" has multiplied, and they have assumed the role of parents in even the most intimate aspects of education. With regard to emotional life, personality and development, rights and duties, these "experts" know everything: objectives, motivations, techniques. And parents must simply listen, learn and adapt. Deprived of their role, they often become overly apprehensive and possessive of their children, to the point of never correcting them: "You cannot correct the child." They tend to entrust them more and more to the "experts," even with regard to the most delicate and personal aspects of their lives, putting themselves on the sidelines; and thus parents today run the risk of excluding themselves from the lives of their children. And this is very serious!

Today there are cases like this. I am not saying that it always happens, but there are cases. The teacher will admonish the child at school and send a note to the parents. I remember a personal case. Once, when I was in the fourth grade, I said a bad word to the teacher, and the teacher, being a good woman, called my mother. She came to school the next day, they spoke together, and then I was called in. And then my mother explained to me in front of the teacher that what I had done was bad, that I shouldn't have done it; but my mother explained with such sweetness and she asked me to apologize to the teacher in front of her. I did it and then I was glad that I had: the story had a happy ending. But that was only the first chapter! When I got home, the second chapter began...

Imagine if today a teacher were to do something like this. The next day the parents, or one of the two, would seek to admonish that teacher, because the "experts" say that children should not be reproached like this. Things have changed! That is why parents should not exclude themselves from their children's education.

It is clear that this approach is not good: it is not harmony, it is not dialogue, and rather than fostering cooperation between the family and other educational agencies, schools, gymnasiums... it counteracts it.

How did we get to this point? There is no doubt that parents or, better yet, certain past educational models had their limitations. There is no doubt. But it is also true that there are mistakes that only parents are allowed to make, because they can compensate for them in a way that is impossible for anyone else. On the other hand, as we well know, life has become stingy with time for talking, reflecting, and facing oneself. Many parents are "sequestered" by work—mother and father have to work—and by worries, uncomfortable with the new needs of their children and with the complexity of modern life—which is the way it is and we must accept it as it is—and they find themselves as if paralyzed by the fear of making a mistake. The problem, however, is not resolved just by talking. Superficial "dialogue" does not lead to a true meeting of mind and heart. Let us ask instead: Do we seek to understand "where" our children really are in their journey? Where is their soul? Do we really know? And, above all: Do we want to know? Are we convinced that they, in reality, aren't waiting for something else?

Christian communities are called to offer support to the educational mission of families, and they do this first of all with the light of the Word of God. The apostle Paul recalls the reciprocity of duties between parents and children: "Children, obey your parents in everything, for this pleases the Lord. Fathers, do not provoke your children, lest they become discouraged" (Col 3:20–21). At the foundation of everything is love, that which God gives us, which "is not arrogant or rude. Love does not insist on its own way; it is not irritable or resentful; it does not rejoice at wrong, but . . . bears all things, believes all things, hopes all things, endures all things" (1 Cor 13:5–7). Even the best families need support, and it takes a lot of patience to support one another! But such is life. Life is not lived in a laboratory, but in reality. Jesus himself experienced a family upbringing.

In this case also, the grace of the love of Christ leads to the fulfillment of what is inscribed in human nature. How many astounding examples we have of Christian parents filled with human wisdom! They show that a good family upbringing is the backbone of humanity. Its radiance in society is the source that allows us to fill in the gaps, wounds, and voids in parenthood that affect less fortunate children. This radiance can work real miracles. And in the Church these miracles happen every day!

I hope that the Lord may bestow on Christian families the faith, freedom, and courage necessary for their mission. If family education rediscovers the pride of its leadership, many things will change for the better, for uncertain parents and for disappointed children. It is time for fathers and mothers to return from their exile—for they have exiled themselves from their children's upbringing—and to fully resume their educational role. We hope that the Lord may give this grace to parents: to not exile themselves from the education of their children. And this can only be done with love, tenderness, and patience.

—*General Audience, Saint Peter's Square, May 20, 2015*

BE CATECHISTS

Teaching the faith is something beautiful! It is perhaps the best legacy we can pass on: the faith! To educate in the faith, to make it grow. To help children, young people and adults to know and love the Lord more and more is one of the most exciting aspects of education. It builds up the Church! To "be" catechists! Not to "work" as catechists: this will not do. I work as a catechist because I like to teach... But unless you "are" a catechist, it is no good! You will not be successful . . . you will not bear fruit! Catechesis is a vocation: "being a catechist," this is the vocation, not working as a catechist. So keep this in mind: I didn't say to do the "work" of catechists, but to "be" catechists, because this is something that embraces our whole life. It means leading people to encounter Christ by our words and our lives, by giving witness. Remember what Benedict XVI said: "The Church does not grow by proselytizing; she grows by attracting others." And what attracts is our witness. Being a catechist means witnessing to the faith, being consistent in our personal life.

This is not easy! We help, we lead others to Jesus with our words and our lives, with our witness. I like to recall what Saint Francis of Assisi used to say to his friars: "Preach the Gospel at all times; if necessary, use words." Words come . . . but witness comes first: people should see the Gospel, read the Gospel, in our lives. To "be" a catechist requires love, an ever stronger love for Christ, a love for his holy people. And this love can't be bought in stores, even in Rome. This love comes from Christ! It is Christ's gift! And if it comes from Christ, it also starts with Christ, and we too need to start anew with Christ, from the love he gives us.

—Address to the International Congress on Catechesis,
September 27, 2013

In the Periphery

God is always ahead of us! When we think about going far away, to the extreme peripheries, we may be a bit afraid, but in fact God is already there. Jesus is waiting for us in the hearts of our brothers and sisters, in their wounded bodies, in their hardships, in their lack of faith. But may I tell you about one of the "peripheries" that breaks my heart? I saw it in my first diocese. It is children who don't even know how to make the sign of the cross. In Buenos Aires there are many children who can't make the sign of the cross. This is one of the "peripheries"! And Jesus is there, waiting for you to help that child make the sign of the cross. Jesus is always there first.

—Address to the International Congress on Catechesis,
September 27, 2013

WE HAVE A RESPONSIBILITY

What are we leaving the children? What example are we setting? Do we teach what we heard in the First Reading: to walk in love and in truth? Or do we teach with words, while our life goes another way? Christians have to take care of kids, of children, and pass on the faith, pass on what they live, what's in their hearts: we can't ignore the little plants that are growing. What is my attitude like? Is it the attitude of a brother, father, mother, or sister who helps the child grow, or is it an attitude of detachment? All of us have a responsibility to give the best we have. And the best we have is the faith: give it to them but give it by example, not with words. Words are useless. Today words are useless. In this world of the image, all of these kids have cell phones, and words are useless. What truly counts is setting an example. Therefore, the decisive question to ask ourselves about the education of the youngest is: what do I give them?

—*Morning homily, November 14, 2014*

THE PLACE OF FORMATION

Education can take place in a variety of settings: at school, in families, in the media, in catechesis, and elsewhere. Good education plants seeds when we are young, and these continue to bear fruit throughout life. Here, though, I would stress the great importance of the family, which is "the place in which life—the gift of God—can be properly welcomed and protected against the many attacks to which it is exposed, and can develop in accordance with what constitutes authentic human growth. In the face of the so-called culture of death, the family is the heart of the culture of life" (John Paul II, *Centesimus Annus*). In the family we first learn how to show love and respect for life. We are taught the proper use of things, order and cleanliness, respect for the local ecosystem and care for all creatures. In the family we receive an integral education, which enables us to grow harmoniously into personal maturity. In the family we learn to ask without demanding, to say "thank you" as an expression of genuine gratitude for what we have been given, to control our aggressivity and greed, and to ask forgiveness when we have caused harm. These simple gestures of heartfelt courtesy help to create a culture of shared life and respect for our surroundings.

—Laudato Si', *213*

AN ASSIGNMENT FOR MOTHERS AND FATHERS

There is something that is very close to my heart, because I have seen it in the city: there are children who have not learned to make the sign of the cross! But you, mother, father, teach your child to pray, to make the sign of the cross: this is a lovely task for mothers and fathers!

—*General Audience, Saint Peter's Square, August 26, 2015*

Admonishing Sinners

DELICACY, PRUDENCE, AND HUMILITY

The gospel this Sunday, taken from Matthew, chapter 18, presents the theme of brotherly correction within the community of believers: that is, how I must correct another Christian when he does what is not good. Jesus teaches us that, should my Christian brother commit a sin against me, offend me, I must be charitable toward him and, first of all, speak with him personally, explain to him what he said or did that was wrong. What if the brother doesn't listen to me? Jesus proposes a progressive intervention: first, return and speak to him with two or three other people, so he may be more aware of his error. If, despite this, he does not accept the admonition, the community must be told, and should he also refuse to listen to the community, he must be made aware of the rift and estrangement that he himself has caused, weakening the communion with his brothers in the faith.

The stages of this plan show the effort that the Lord asks of his community in order to accompany the one who transgresses, so that he or she is not lost. It is important above all to prevent any clamor in the news and gossip in the community...

The approach is one of sensitivity, prudence, humility, attention toward the one who committed a fault in order to avoid wounding or killing the brother with words. Because, you know, words too can kill! When I speak, when I make an unfair criticism, when I "flay" a brother with my tongue, this is killing another person's reputation! Words kill too. Let us pay attention to this. At the same time, the discretion of speaking to him alone is to avoid needlessly humiliating the sinner. It is discussed between the two, no one is aware of it, and then it's over…

The purpose is to help the person realize what he has done, and that through his fault he has offended not only one, but everyone. But it also helps us to free ourselves from anger or resentment, which only causes harm—that bitterness of heart which brings anger and resentment, and which leads us to insult and aggression. It is terrible to see an insult or taunt issue from the mouth of a Christian. It is ugly. Do you understand? Do not insult! To insult is not Christian. Understood? To insult is not Christian.

Actually, before God we are all sinners and in need of forgiveness. All of us. Indeed, Jesus told us not to judge. Fraternal correction is a mark of the love and communion which must reign in the Christian community. It is a mutual service that we can and must render to one another. To reprove a brother is a service, and it is possible and effective only if each one recognizes oneself to be a as sinner and in need of the Lord's forgiveness. The same awareness that enables me to recognize the fault of another, even before that, reminds me that I have likewise made mistakes and I am often wrong.

—Angelus, *September 7, 2014*

FRATERNAL CORRECTION

Christians risk disqualification, as Saint Paul admonishes, if they insist on performing brotherly correction without charity, truth, and humility, making room for hypocrisy and gossip. In fact this service to others requires one, first of all, to recognize oneself as a sinner and not to sit in judgment.

Today the Lord makes us consider one of these approaches, which he has already spoken of, and that is brotherly correction. The bottom line is: when a brother, a sister from the community makes a mistake, how does one correct that person?

Through the readings of the liturgy (Lk 6:39–42) the Lord has given us advice on how to correct others. We must correct him or her, but we must do it as someone who sees and not as one who is blind. "Can a blind man lead a blind man?"

Thus to offer correction it is necessary to see clearly and to follow several rules of behavior that the Lord himself proposes. First of all, the advice he gives to correct a brother we heard the other day. It is to take aside your brother who made the error and speak to him, telling him, "Brother, in this regard, I believe you did not do right!"

And to take him aside, indeed, means to correct him with charity. Otherwise, it would be like performing surgery without anesthesia, resulting in a patient's painful death. And charity is like anesthesia that helps him to receive the care and to accept the correction. Here then is the first step toward a brother: take him aside, gently, lovingly, and speak to him.

Along with charity, it is necessary to tell the truth and never say something that is not true. Many times in our communities things are said to another person that aren't true: they are libelous. Or, if they are true, they harm the reputation of that person.

Jesus speaks of the third rule, humility, in the passage of Luke's Gospel: correct others without hypocrisy, that is, with humility. It is good to consider that if you must correct a tiny flaw in someone else, you must be aware that you have so many that are greater. The Lord says this effectively: first take the log out of your own eye, and then you will see clearly to take out the speck from the eye of another. Only in this way will you not be blind and will you see clearly to truly help your brother. Thus humility is important in order to recognize that I am a greater sinner than he, a greater sinner than she. Afterwards I must help him or her to correct this flaw.

If I do not perform brotherly correction with charity, do not perform it in truth, and do not perform it with humility, I become blind. And if I do not see, how do I heal another blind person?

Fraternal correction is an act to heal the body of the Church. It is like mending a hole in the fabric of the Church. However, one must proceed with much sensitivity, like mothers and grandmothers when they mend, and this is the very manner in which one must perform brotherly correction.

On the other hand, if you are not capable of performing fraternal reproof with love, with charity, in truth and with humility, you will offend and cause damage to that person's heart. You will wound, and you will become a blind hypocrite, as Jesus says. Indeed, the day's reading from the Gospel of Luke reads: "You hypocrite, first take the log out of your eye."

There is a sign that perhaps can help us: when one sees something wrong and feels that he should correct it but perceives a certain pleasure in doing so, then it is time to pay attention, because that is not the Lord's way. Indeed, in the Lord there is always the cross, the difficulty of doing something good. And love and gentleness always come from the Lord.

—*Morning homily, September 12, 2014*

A Way of Doing Justice

There is another way of doing justice, which the Bible presents to us as the royal road to take. It is a process that avoids recourse to the tribunal and allows the victim to face the culprit directly and invite him or her to conversion, helping the person to understand that they are doing evil, and thus appealing to their conscience. In this way, by finally repenting and acknowledging their wrong, they can open themselves to the forgiveness that the injured party is offering them. And this is beautiful: after being persuaded that what was done was wrong, the heart opens to the forgiveness being offered to it. This is the way to resolve conflicts in the family, in the relationship between spouses or between parents and children, where the offended party loves the guilty one and wishes to save the bond that unites them. Do not sever that bond, that relationship.

—*General Audience, Saint Peter's Square, February 4, 2015*

Our First Neighbor

Closeness! Who is the first neighbor of a consecrated man or woman? The brother or sister in the community. This is your first neighbor. A kind, good, loving closeness too. I know that in your communities there is never gossip, never, ever... A way of distancing oneself [is] to gossip. Listen carefully: no gossip, the terrorism of gossip. Because those who gossip are terrorists. They are terrorists in their own community, because like a bomb they drop a word against this one or that one, and then they go calmly. Those who do this destroy, like a bomb, and they distance themselves. This, the apostle James said, is perhaps the most difficult virtue, the most difficult human and spiritual virtue to have, that of bridling the tongue. If it occurs to you to say something against a brother or sister, to drop a bomb of gossip, bite your tongue! Hard! No terrorism in the community! "But Father, what if there is something, a defect, something to correct?" You say it to the person: "You have an attitude that bothers me, or that isn't good." If this isn't appropriate—because sometimes it isn't prudent—you say it to the person who can remedy, who can resolve the problem, and to no one else. Understood? Gossip is useless. "But in the chapter house?" There, yes! In public, say what you feel you have to say, because there is temptation not to say things in the chapter house, and then outside: "Did you see the prioress? Did you see the abbess? Did you see the mother superior?..." Why didn't you say it there in the chapter house?... Is this clear? This is a virtue of proximity. The saints, the consecrated saints had this virtue. Saint

Thérèse of the Child Jesus never, ever, complained about work, about the bother it was to bring that sister to the dining room every evening: from the choir to the dining room. Never! Because that poor nun was very old, almost paralyzed, she had difficulty walking, she was in pain—I understand her too!—she was even a bit neurotic...Never, ever did Saint Thérèse go to another sister to say: "How she bothers me!" What did she do? She helped her sit down, brought her a napkin, broke the bread, and did so with a smile. This is called proximity. Closeness! If you drop the bomb of gossip in your community, this is not closeness: this is waging war! This is distancing yourself, this is creating distance, creating anarchy in the community. In this Year of Mercy, if each one of you could manage to never be a gossiping terrorist, it would be a success for the Church, a success of great holiness! Take courage! Proximity.

—*Address to participants in the Jubilee for Consecrated Life,*
Vatican City, February 1, 2016

Consoling the Afflicted

He Walks Beside Us

Let us think of the two disciples on the way to Emmaus: their sad faces, their barren journey, their despair. But Jesus does not abandon them. He walks beside them, and not only that! Patiently he explains the scriptures which spoke of him, and he stays to share a meal with them.

This is God's way of doing things. He is not impatient like us, who often want everything all at once, even in our dealings with other people. God is patient with us because he loves us, and those who love are able to understand, to hope, to inspire confidence. They do not give up, they do not burn bridges, they are able to forgive.

Let us remember this in our lives as Christians: God always waits for us, even when we have left him behind! He is never far from us, and if we return to him, he is ready to embrace us.

—Homily, Mass for the Possession of the Chair of the Bishop of Rome, February 1, 2016

THE GIFT OF PIETY

If the gift of piety makes us grow in relation to and in communion with God and leads us to live as his children, at the same time, it helps us *to pass this love on to others as well and to recognize them as our brothers and sisters*. And then, yes, we will be moved by feelings of piety—not pietism!—in relation to those around us and to those whom we encounter every day. Why do I say "not pietism"? Because some think that to be pious is to close one's eyes, to pose like a picture and pretend to be a saint. In Piedmont we say: to play the "mugna quacia" [literally: the pious or serene nun]. This is not the gift of piety. The gift of piety means to be truly capable of rejoicing with those who rejoice, of weeping with those who weep, of being close to those who are lonely or in anguish, of correcting those in error, of consoling the afflicted, of welcoming and helping those in need. The gift of piety is closely tied to gentleness. The gift of piety which the Holy Spirit gives us makes us gentle, makes us calm, patient, at peace with God, at the service of others with gentleness.

Dear friends, in the letter to the Romans the apostle Paul states: "For all who are led by the Spirit of God are sons of God. For you did not receive the spirit of slavery to fall back into fear, but you have received the spirit of sonship," from which "we cry, 'Abba! Father!'" (Rm 8:14–15). Let us ask the Lord for the gift of his Spirit to conquer our fear, our uncertainty, and our restless, impatient spirit, and to make of us joyful witnesses of God and of his love, by worshiping the Lord in truth and in service to our neighbor with gentleness and with a smile, which the Holy Spirit al-

ways gives us in joy. May the Holy Spirit grant to all of us
this gift of piety.

—*General Audience, Saint Peter's Square, June 4, 2014*

CONSOLE MY PEOPLE

This Sunday marks the second stage of the season of Advent, a marvelous time that reawakens in us the expectation
of Christ's return and the memory of his historical coming.
Today's liturgy presents us with a message full of hope. It is
the Lord's express invitation from the lips of the prophet
Isaiah: "Comfort, comfort my people, says your God" (40:1).
These words open the *Book of Comfort*, in which the prophet
announces the joyous proclamation of liberation to the people in exile. The time of tribulation has ended. The people of
Israel can look trustingly toward the future: at last they can
return to their homeland. This is the reason for the invitation
to let themselves be comforted by the Lord.

Isaiah addresses people who have passed through a
dark period, who have been subjected to a very difficult
trial; now the time of comfort has come. Sorrow and fear
can be replaced with joy, for the Lord himself will guide his
people on the way to liberation and salvation. How will he
do all this? With the solicitude and tenderness of a shepherd who takes care of his flock. He will in fact provide
unity and security and feed his flock, gather the lost sheep
into his sure fold, reserve special attention for the most
fragile and weak (v. 11). This is God's attitude toward us,
his creatures. For this reason, the prophet invites those who
hear him—including us, today—to spread this message of

hope: that the Lord consoles us, and that we are to make room for the comfort that comes from the Lord.

We cannot be messengers of God's comfort if we do not first feel the joy of being comforted and loved by him. This happens especially when we hear his word, the Gospel, which we should carry in our pocket: do not forget this! The Gospel in your pocket or purse, to read regularly. And this gives us comfort: when we abide in silent prayer in his presence, when we encounter him in the Eucharist or in the sacrament of reconciliation. All this comforts us.

Let us therefore allow Isaiah's call—"Comfort, comfort my people"—to resound in our heart in this season of Advent. Today there is need for people to be witnesses to the mercy and tenderness of God, who spurs the resigned, enlivens the disheartened, ignites the fire of hope. He ignites the fire of hope! We don't. So many situations require our comforting witness, to be joyful, comforting people. I am thinking of those who are burdened by suffering, injustice, and tyranny, of those who are slaves to money, to power, to success, to worldliness. Poor sufferers! They have fake consolations, not the true comfort of the Lord! We are all called to comfort our brothers and sisters, to testify that God alone can eliminate the causes of existential and spiritual tragedies. He can do it! He is powerful!

Isaiah's message, which resounds on this second Sunday of Advent, is a salve to our wounds and an impetus to prepare the way of the Lord. Indeed, today the prophet speaks to our hearts to tell us that God forgives our sins and comforts us. If we entrust ourselves to him with a humble and penitent heart, he will tear down the walls of evil, he will fill in the holes of our omissions, he will smooth over the bumps of arrogance and vanity, and he will open the way to encounter with him. It is curious, but many times we are afraid of consolation, of being comforted. Or rather, we feel more secure in sorrow and desolation. Do you know why? Because in sorrow we feel almost like protagonists. However, in consolation the Holy Spirit is the protagonist! It is he who consoles us, it is he who gives us the courage to go out of ourselves. It is he who opens the door to the source of every true comfort, which is the Father. And this is conversion. Please, let yourselves be comforted by the Lord! Let yourselves be comforted by the Lord!

—Angelus, *December 7, 2014*

True Joy

The human heart desires joy. We all desire joy. Every family, every people aspires to happiness. But what is the joy that the Christian is called to live out and bear witness to? It is the joy that comes from the *closeness of God*, from his *presence* in our life. From the moment Jesus entered into history, with his birth in Bethlehem, humanity received the seed of the Kingdom of God as the soil receives the seed, the promise of a future harvest. There is no need to look further! Jesus has come to bring joy to all people for all time. It is not just a hopeful joy or a joy postponed until paradise, as if here on earth we are sad but in paradise we will be filled with joy. No! It is not that, but a joy already real and tangible now, because *Jesus himself is our joy*, and with Jesus joy finds its home, as your sign there says: joy is at home in Jesus. All of us, let us say it: "Joy is at home in Jesus." Once more: "Joy is at home in Jesus." And without Jesus is there joy? No! Well done! He is living, he is the Risen One, and he works in us and among us especially with the word and the sacraments.

We who are baptized, children of the Church, we are called to accept ever anew the presence of God among us and to help others to discover him, or to rediscover what they have forgotten. It is a most beautiful mission, like that of John the Baptist: to direct the people to Christ—not to ourselves!—for he is the destination to which the human heart tends when it seeks joy and happiness.

In today's liturgy Saint Paul again indicates the conditions for being "missionaries of joy": praying constantly, always giving thanks to God, giving way to his Spirit, seeking the good and avoiding evil (cf. 1 Thess 5:17–22). If this becomes our lifestyle, then the Good News will be able to enter so many homes and help people and families to rediscover that in Jesus lies salvation. In him it is possible to find interior peace and the strength to face different life situations every day, even in the situations that are heaviest and most difficult. No one has ever heard of a sad saint with a mournful face. This is unheard of! It would be a contradiction. The Christian's heart is filled with peace because he knows how to place his joy in the Lord even when going through the difficult moments in life. To have faith does not mean to never have difficult moments but to have the strength to face those moments knowing that we are not alone. And this is the peace that God gives to his children.

With her gaze turned to Christmas already close at hand, the Church invites us to bear witness to the fact that

Jesus is not a person of the past; he is the Word of God who today continues to illuminate the path of mankind; his gestures—the sacraments—are the manifestation of the tenderness, consolation, and love that the Father bears for every human being. May the Virgin Mary, "Cause of our joy," render us ever more joyous in the Lord, who comes to free us from the many forms of interior and exterior slavery.

—Angelus, *December 14, 2014*

LIGHT IN THE DARKNESS

We proclaim the resurrection of Christ when his light illumines the dark moments of our life and we can share that with others, when we know how to smile with those who smile and weep with those who weep, when we walk beside those who are sad and in danger of losing hope, when we share our experience of faith with those who are searching for meaning and for happiness. With our attitude, with our witness, with our life, we say: Jesus is risen! Let us say it with all our soul.

—Regina Caeli, *April 6, 2015*

KEEPING HOPE ALIVE

I am moved when I see many mothers carrying their children on their shoulders. Like so many of you here! Carrying your children, you bring your lives and the future of your people. You bring all your joys and hopes. You bring the blessing of the earth and all its fruits. You bring the work of your hands, hands that work today in order to weave tomorrow's hopes and dreams. But those shoulders are also weighed down by bitter disappointments and sorrows, scarred by experiences of injustice and of justice denied ...

Frequently we tire of this journey. Frequently we lack the strength to keep hope alive. How often have we experienced situations that dull our memory, weaken our hope, and make us lose our reason for rejoicing! And then a kind of sadness takes over. We think only of ourselves, we forget that we are a people that is loved, a chosen people. And the loss of that memory disorients us, it closes our heart to others, and especially to the poor.

We may feel the way the disciples did, when they saw those crowds of people gathered there. They begged Jesus to send them away—"send them home"—since it was impossible to provide food for so many people. Faced with so many kinds of hunger in our world, we can say to ourselves: "Sorry, but things don't add up; we will never manage, there is nothing to be done." And so our hearts yield to despair.

A despairing heart finds it easy to succumb to a way of thinking that is becoming ever more widespread in our world today. It is a mentality in which everything has a price, everything can be bought, everything is negotiable. This way of thinking has room only for a select few, while it discards all those who are "unproductive," unsuitable, or unworthy, since clearly those people don't "measure up." But Jesus once more turns to us and says: "No, no, they don't need to be excluded, they don't need to go away; you yourselves, give them something to eat."

Those words of Jesus have a particular resonance for us today. No one needs to be excluded, no one has to be discarded. *You yourselves*, give them something to eat. Jesus speaks these words to us, here in this square. Yes, no one has to be discarded; *you*, give them something to eat. Jesus' way of seeing things leaves no room for the mentality that would cut off the weak and those most in need. Taking the lead, he gives us his own example, he shows us the way forward. What he does can be summed up in three words. He *takes* a little bread and some fish, he *blesses* them, and then *gives* them to his disciples to share with the crowd. And this is how the miracle takes place. It is not magic or sorcery. With these three gestures, Jesus is able to turn a mentality that discards others into a mindset of communion, a mindset of community.

—*Homily, Santa Cruz de la Sierra, Bolivia, July 9, 2015*

LOAVES AND FISHES

Before the suffering, loneliness, poverty, and difficulties of so many people, what can we ourselves do? Complaining doesn't resolve anything, but we can offer the little that we have, like the boy in the Gospel. We surely have a few hours of time, certain talents, some skills...Who among us doesn't have "five loaves and two fish" of his own? We all have them! If we are willing to place them in the Lord's hands, they will be enough to bring about a little more love, peace, justice, and especially joy in the world. How necessary joy is in the world! God is capable of multiplying our small acts of solidarity and allowing us to share in his gift.

—*Angelus, July 26, 2015*

The Presence of God

I would like to pause above all on joy. The true joy that is experienced in the family is not something random and casual. It is a joy produced by deep harmony among people, which allows them to savor the beauty of being together, of supporting each other on life's journey. However, at the foundation of joy there is always the presence of God, his welcoming, merciful, and patient love for all. If the door of the family is not open to the presence of God and to his love, then the family loses its harmony, individualism prevails, and joy is extinguished. Instead, the family that experiences joy—the joy of life, the joy of faith—communicates it spontaneously, is the salt of the earth and the light of the world, the leaven for all of society.

—Angelus, *December 27, 2015*

Pardoning Offenses

WE ARE NOT NUMBERS

I am always struck when I reread the parable of the merciful father. It impresses me because it always gives me great hope. Think of that younger son who was in the father's house, who was loved. And yet he wanted his part of the inheritance. He went off, spent everything, hit rock bottom, where he could not be more distant from his father, yet when he was at his lowest, he missed the warmth of the father's house and he went back.

And the father? Had he forgotten the son? No, never. He is there, he sees the son from afar, he has been waiting for him every hour of every day, the son has always been in his father's heart, even though he left him, even though he squandered his whole inheritance, his freedom. The father, with patience, love, hope, and mercy, has never for a second stopped thinking about him, and as soon as he sees him still far off, he runs out to meet him and embraces him with tenderness, the tenderness of God, without a word of reproach: he has returned! And that is the joy of the father. In that embrace for his son is all this joy: he has returned! . . .

149

Maybe someone among us here is thinking: my sin is so great, I am as far from God as the younger son in the parable, my unbelief is like that of Thomas; I don't have the courage to go back, to believe that God can welcome me and that he is waiting for me, of all people. But God is indeed waiting for you. He asks of you only the courage to go to him.

How many times in my pastoral ministry have I heard it said: "Father, I have many sins"; and I have always pleaded: "Don't be afraid, go to him, he is waiting for you, he will take care of everything." We hear many offers from the world around us, but let us take up God's offer instead: his is a caress of love. For God, we are not numbers, we are important, indeed we are the most important thing to him; even if we are sinners, we are what is closest to his heart...

In my own life, I have so often seen God's merciful countenance, his patience. I have also seen so many people find the courage to enter the wounds of Jesus by saying to him: Lord, I am here, accept my poverty, hide my sin in your wounds, wash it away with your blood. And I have always seen that God did just this—he accepted them, consoled them, cleansed them, loved them.

Dear brothers and sisters, let us be enveloped by the mercy of God. Let us trust in his patience, which always gives us more time. Let us find the courage to return to his house, to dwell in his loving wounds, allowing ourselves be loved by him and to encounter his mercy in the sacraments. We will feel his wonderful tenderness, we will feel his embrace, and we too will become more capable of mercy, patience, forgiveness, and love.

—Homily, Papal Mass for the Possession of the Chair of Peter,
April 7, 2013

THAT THEY MAY BE ONE

Clearly we cannot deny the divisions that continue to exist among us, the disciples of Jesus. This sacred place makes us even more painfully aware of how tragic they are. And yet, fifty years after the embrace of those two venerable fathers [Pope Paul VI and Patriarch Athenagoras], we realize with gratitude and renewed amazement how it was possible, at the prompting of the Holy Spirit, to take truly significant steps toward unity. We know that much distance still needs to be traveled before we attain that fullness of communion which can also be expressed by sharing the same eucharistic table, something we ardently desire. Yet our disagreements must not frighten us and paralyze our progress. We need to believe that, just as the stone before the tomb was cast aside, so too every obstacle to our full communion will also be removed. This will be a grace of resurrection, of which we can have a foretaste even today. Every time we ask forgiveness of one another for our sins against other Christians and every time we find the courage to grant and receive such forgiveness, we experience the resurrection! Every time we put behind us our longstanding prejudices and find the courage to build new fraternal relationships, we confess that Christ is truly risen! Every time we reflect on the future of the Church in the light of her vocation to unity, the dawn of Easter breaks forth! Here I reiterate the hope already expressed by my predecessors for a continued dialogue with all our brothers and sisters in Christ, aimed at finding a means of exercising the specific ministry of the bishop of Rome which, in fidelity to his mission, can be open to a new situation and can be, in the present context, a service of love and of communion acknowledged by all (cf. John Paul II, *Ut Unum Sint*, 95–96).

—*Ecumenical Celebration on the occasion of the fiftieth anniversary of the meeting between Pope Paul VI and Patriarch Athenagoras in Jerusalem, May 25, 2014*

THE POWER OF THE CROSS

The first reading presents God's promise to restore to unity and prosperity a people dispersed by disaster and division. For us, as for the people of Israel, this is a promise full of hope: it points to a future that God is even now preparing for us. Yet this promise is inseparably tied to a command: the command to return to God and wholeheartedly obey his law (cf. Dt 30:2–3). God's gifts of reconciliation, unity, and peace are inseparably linked to the grace of conversion, a change of heart that can alter the course of our lives and our history, as individuals and as a people.

At this Mass, we naturally hear this promise in the context of the historical experience of the Korean people, an experience of division and conflict that has lasted for well over sixty years. But God's urgent summons to conversion also challenges Christ's followers in Korea to examine the quality of their own contribution to the building of a truly just and humane society. It challenges each of you to reflect on the extent to which you, as individuals and communities, show evangelical concern for the less fortunate, the marginalized, those without work, and those who do not share in the prosperity of the many. And it challenges you, as Christians and Koreans, firmly to reject a mindset shaped by suspicion, confrontation, and competition, and instead to shape a culture formed by the teaching of the Gospel and the noblest traditional values of the Korean people...

Jesus asks us to believe that forgiveness is the door that leads to reconciliation. In telling us to forgive our brothers unreservedly, he is asking us to do something utterly radical, but he also gives us the grace to do it. What appears, from a human perspective, to be impossible, impractical, and even at times repugnant, he makes possible and fruitful through the infinite power of his cross. The cross of Christ reveals the power of God to bridge every division, to heal every wound, and to reestablish the original bonds of brotherly love.

This, then, is the message that I leave you as I conclude my visit to Korea. Trust in the power of Christ's cross! Welcome its reconciling grace into your own hearts and share that grace with others! I ask you to bear convincing witness to Christ's message of reconciliation in your homes, in your communities, and at every level of national life. I am confident that, in a spirit of friendship and cooperation with other Christians, with the followers of other religions, and with all men and women of good will concerned for the future of Korean society, you will be a leaven of the Kingdom of God in this land. Thus our prayers for peace and reconciliation will rise to God from ever more pure hearts and, by his gracious gift, obtain that precious good for which we all long.

Let us pray, then, for the emergence of new opportunities for dialogue, encounter, and the resolution of differences, for continued generosity in providing humanitarian assistance to those in need, and for an ever greater recognition that all

Koreans are brothers and sisters, members of one family, one people. They speak the same language.

—*Homily, Mass for Peace and Reconciliation, Seoul, South Korea, August 18, 2014*

THE MEMORY OF THE MARTYRS

Today, like yesterday, the strength of the Church does not stem so much from organizational capabilities or structures, which are also necessary: the strength of the Church does not lie there. Our strength is Christ's love! It is a strength that sustains us in moments of difficulty and that inspires everyday apostolic action in order to offer goodness and forgiveness to everyone, thereby witnessing to the mercy of God.

Travelling [in Albania] along Tirana's principal boulevard that leads from the airport to the great central square, I was able to glimpse the portraits of forty priests assassinated during the communist dictatorship, for whom the cause of beatification has been opened. These are joined by hundreds of Christian and Muslim religious men and women assassinated, tortured, imprisoned, and deported simply because they believed in God. There were dark years during which religious freedom was razed to the ground and belief in God was prohibited. Thousands of churches and mosques were destroyed, transformed into warehouses and cinemas that propagated the Marxist ideology. Religious books were burned, and parents were prohibited from giving their children the religious names of their ancestors. The memory of such tragic events is essential for the future of a people. The memory of martyrs who resisted in faith is a guarantee for the future of Albania, because their blood was not shed in vain, but is a seed that will bear the fruit of peace and fraternal cooperation. Today, in fact, Albania is an example not only of the rebirth of the Church, but also of the peaceful coexistence of religions. Thus, the martyrs are not the defeated but the victors: resplendent in their heroic witness is the omnipotence of God who always comforts his people, opening new paths and horizons of hope.

—General Audience, Saint Peter's Square, September 24, 2014

HAVE MERCY ON ME, LORD

At the beginning of Mass, every Mass, we are called before the Lord to recognize that we are sinners, expressing through words and gestures sincere repentance of the heart. And we say: "Have mercy on me, Lord. I am a sinner! I confess to Almighty God my sins." And we don't say: "Lord, have mercy on this man who is beside me, or this woman, who are sinners." No! "Have mercy on me!" We are all sinners and in need of the Lord's forgiveness. It is the Holy Spirit who speaks to our spirit and makes us recognize our faults in light of the Word of Jesus. Jesus himself invites us all, saints and sinners, to his table, gathering us from the crossroads, from diverse situations of life (cf. Mt 22:9–10). And among the conditions in common among those participating in the eucharistic celebration, two are fundamental in order to go to Mass correctly: we are all sinners and God grants his mercy to all. These are the two conditions that open wide the doors that we might enter Mass properly. We must always remember this before addressing a brother in brotherly correction.

—Angelus, *September 7, 2014*

TRANSFORMING OUR LIFE

The Eucharist is Jesus himself who gives himself entirely to us. *Nourishing ourselves* with him and *abiding* with him through eucharistic communion, if we do so with faith, *transforms our life*, transforms it into a gift to God and to our brothers and sisters. Nourishing ourselves with that "Bread of Life" means entering into harmony with the heart of Christ, assimilating his choices, his thoughts, his behavior. It means entering into a dynamism of love and becoming people of peace, people of forgiveness, people of reconciliation, people of sharing in solidarity—people like Jesus.

—Angelus, *August 16, 2015*

FORGIVENESS IN THE FAMILY

Today, I would like to emphasize that the family is a great *training ground for the mutual giving and forgiving* without which no love can last for long. Without self-giving and seeking forgiveness love does not last, it does not endure. In the prayer that he himself taught us—the Our Father— Jesus tells us to ask the Father: "*Forgive us our debts, as we also have forgiven our debtors.*" And at the end he states: "For if you forgive men their trespasses, your heavenly Father also will forgive you; but if you do not forgive men their trespasses, neither will your Father forgive your trespasses" (Mt 6:12, 14–15).

One cannot live without seeking forgiveness, or at least, one cannot live at peace, especially in the family. We wrong one another every day. We must take into account these mistakes caused by our frailty and our selfishness. However, what we are asked to do is to promptly heal the wounds that we cause, to immediately reweave the bonds that have been broken within the family. If we wait too long, everything becomes more difficult. There is a simple secret to healing wounds and avoiding recriminations. It is this: do not let the day end without apologizing, without making peace between husband and wife, between parents and children, between brothers and sisters ... between daughters-in-law and mothers-in-law! If we learn to apologize promptly and to offer each other mutual forgiveness, the wounds heal, the marriage grows stronger, and the family becomes an increasingly stronger home that can withstand the shocks of our smaller or greater misdeeds. This is why there is no need for a long speech, as a caress is enough: one caress and everything is over and one can start afresh. But do not end the day at war!

If we learn to live this way in the family, we can also do so outside the family, wherever we may be. It is easy to be skeptical about this. Many people—even Christians—think it is an exaggeration. It is said: yes, they are fine words, but it is impossible to put them into practice. But thanks be to God it is not so. Indeed, it is precisely in receiving forgiveness from God that we in turn are capable of forgiving others. This is why Jesus has us repeat these words each time we recite the Our Father, that is, every day. And it is crucial that, in a sometimes pitiless society, there be places, such as the family, in which we can learn to forgive one another.

The synod has rekindled our hope in this regard: namely, that the capacity to forgive and to seek forgiveness is part of the vocation and the mission of the family. Practicing forgiveness not only saves families from divisiveness, but makes them capable of helping society to be less heartless and less cruel. Yes, each act of forgiveness fixes the cracks in the house and strengthens its walls. The Church, dear families, is always beside you to help you build your house on the rock that Jesus spoke of. Let us not forget these words that immediately preceded the parable of the house: "Not every one who says to me, 'Lord, Lord' shall enter the kingdom of heaven, but he who does the will of my Father who is in heaven." And he adds: "On that day many will say to me, 'Lord, Lord, did we not prophesy in your name, and cast out demons in your name...?' And then will I declare to them, 'I never knew you'" (Mt 7:21–23). It is undoubtedly a strong message, with the purpose of shaking us and calling us to convert.

I assure you, dear families, that if you are capable of walking ever more firmly on the path of the beatitudes, learning and teaching to mutually forgive each other, the capacity to bear witness to the renewing power of God's forgiveness will grow in the whole of the great family of the Church. Conversely, even though we may make beautiful sermons and perhaps drive away some demons, in the end the Lord will not recognize us as his disciples if we do not have the capacity to forgive and ask others to forgive us!

Truly Christian families can do a great deal for today's society, and also for the Church. For this reason I hope that in the Jubilee of Mercy families may rediscover the treasure of mutual forgiveness. Let us pray that families may be ever more capable of experiencing and building practical paths of reconciliation where no one feels abandoned to the weight of his or her debts.

—*General Audience, Saint Peter's Square, November 4, 2015*

What Christ Feels

Is it true that in the various situations and circumstances of life we have within us the same feelings that Jesus has? Is it true that we feel as Christ feels? For example, when we suffer some wrongdoing or some insult, do we manage to react without animosity and to forgive from the heart those who apologize to us? How difficult it is to forgive! How difficult! "You're going to pay for this"—that phrase comes from inside! When we are called to share joys or sorrows, do we know how to sincerely weep with those who weep and rejoice with those who rejoice? When we should express our faith, do we know how to do it with courage and simplicity, without being ashamed of the Gospel? Thus we can ask ourselves so many questions. We're not all right. We must always convert and have the sentiments that Jesus had.

—Angelus, *December 6, 2015*

Icon of Divine Mercy

The Immaculate Conception signifies that Mary is the first one to be saved by the infinite mercy of the Father, as the first fruit of the salvation that God wills to give to every man and woman in Christ. For this reason the Immaculate One has become the sublime icon of the divine mercy which has conquered sin. Today, at the beginning of the Jubilee of Mercy, we want to look to this icon with trusting love and to contemplate her in all her splendor, emulating her faith.

In the Immaculate Conception of Mary we are invited to recognize the dawn of the new world, transformed by the salvific work of the Father and of the Son and of the Holy Spirit, the dawn of the new creation brought about by divine mercy. For this reason the Virgin Mary, never tainted by sin and always full of God, is the mother of a new humanity. She is the mother of the recreated world.

Celebrating this feast entails two things. First: fully welcoming God and his merciful grace into our life. Second: becoming in our turn artisans of mercy by means of an evangelical journey. The Feast of the Immaculate Conception then becomes the feast of all of us if, with our daily "yes," we manage to overcome our selfishness and make the life of our brothers ever more glad, to give them hope by drying a few tears and giving a bit of joy. In imitation of Mary we are called to become bearers of Christ and witnesses to his love, looking first of all to those who are privileged in the eyes of Jesus. They are the ones whom he himself indicated: "I was hungry and you gave me food, I was thirsty and you gave me drink, I was a stranger and you welcomed me, I was naked and you clothed me, I was sick and you visited me, I was in prison and you came to me" (Mt 25:35-36).

Today's feast of the Immaculate Conception has a specific message for us: it reminds us that in our life everything is a gift, it is all mercy. May the Blessed Virgin, first fruit of the saved, model of the Church, holy and immaculate spouse, loved by the Lord, help us to ever increasingly re-discover divine mercy as the distinguishing mark of Christians. One cannot understand a true Christian who is not merciful, just as one cannot comprehend God without his mercy. This is the word that epitomizes the Gospel: mercy. It is the fundamental feature of the face of Christ, that face that we recognize in the various aspects of his ex-istence: when he goes to meet everyone, when he heals the sick, when he sits at table with sinners, and above all when, nailed to the cross, he forgives; there we see the face of di-vine mercy. Let us not be afraid: let us allow ourselves to be embraced by the mercy of God who awaits us and forgives all. Nothing is sweeter than his mercy. Let us allow our-selves to be caressed by God: the Lord is so good, and he forgives all.

—Angelus, *Solemnity of the Immaculate Conception,*
December 8, 2015

Born by the Forgiveness of God

Today we celebrate the Feast of Saint Stephen. The remem-brance of the first martyr follows immediately after the solemnity of Christmas. Yesterday we contemplated the merciful love of God, who became flesh for us. Today we see the fitting response of Jesus' disciple, who gives his life. Yesterday the Savior was born on earth; today his faithful servant is born in heaven. Yesterday, as today, the shadows of the rejection of life appear, but the light of love—which conquers hatred and inaugurates a new world—shines even brighter.

There is a special aspect of today's account from the Acts of the Apostles that brings Saint Stephen close to the Lord. It is his *forgiveness before* he is stoned to *death*. Nailed to the cross, Jesus said, "Father, forgive them; for they know not what they do" (Lk 23:34). Likewise, Stephen "knelt down and cried out with a loud voice, 'Lord, do not hold this sin against them'" (Acts 7:60). Stephen is therefore a *martyr, which means witness, because he does as Jesus did.* Indeed, true witnesses are those who act as Jesus did: those who pray, who love, who give, but above all who *forgive,* because forgiveness, as the word itself says, is the highest expression of giving.

We could ask, however, what good is it to forgive? Is it merely a good deed or does it bring results? We find an answer in the very martyrdom of Stephen. Among those for whom he implores forgiveness there is a young man named Saul; this man persecuted the Church and tried to destroy it (cf. Acts 8:3). Shortly thereafter Saul becomes Paul, the great saint, the apostle of the people. He has received Stephen's forgiveness. We could say that Paul is born by the grace of God and by Stephen's forgiveness.

We too *are born by the forgiveness of God.* Not only in baptism, but each time we are forgiven our heart is reborn, it is *renewed.* With each step forward in the life of faith the sign of divine mercy is imprinted anew, for only when we are loved are we in turn able to love. Let us remember this, it will be good for us: if we wish to progress in faith, first of all we must receive God's forgiveness; we must meet the Father, who is willing to forgive all things, always, and who precisely in forgiving heals the heart and rekindles love. We must never tire of asking for divine forgiveness, because only when we are forgiven, when we feel we are forgiven, do we learn to forgive.

Forgiving, however, is not an easy thing; it is always very difficult. How can we imitate Jesus? From what point do we begin to pardon the small and great wrongs that we suffer each day? First of all, we begin *with prayer, as St. Stephen did*. We begin with our own heart: with prayer we are able to face the resentment we feel *by entrusting to God's mercy those who have wronged us*: "Lord, I pray for him, I pray for her." Then we discover that this inner struggle to forgive cleanses us of evil, and that prayer and love free us from the interior chains of bitterness. It is so awful to live in bitterness! Every day we have the opportunity to practice forgiving, to live a gesture so lofty that it brings us closer to God. Like our heavenly Father, may we too become merciful, because through forgiveness, *we conquer evil with good*, we transform hatred into love, and in this way we help to cleanse the world.

—Angelus, *Feast of Saint Stephen, Proto-martyr, December 26, 2015*

Bearing Wrongs Patiently

In showing patience to those who wrong us and, by extension, to those we find irritating, we imitate God's own patience with us sinners. Exercising patience with others also challenges us to reflect on our own conduct and failings. Patience is also required in two related spiritual works of mercy: admonishing sinners and instructing the ignorant. We think of the patience shown by the many parents, catechists, and teachers who quietly help young people to grow in faith and knowledge of the important things in life. Helping others to look past the ephemeral, to discover the Lord's will in their lives and thus to find lasting joy, is a great act of charity. By serving our brothers and sisters in this way, our own minds and hearts are purified and renewed.

May the Holy Spirit grant us the generosity and patience we need to support and encourage those around us, so that together we may cherish the things that truly matter.

—General Audience, Saint Peter's Square, November 16, 2016

LOVE IS GREATER

The Word of God calls us to love one another, even if we do not always understand each other, and do not always get along... it is then that Christian love is seen. It is a love that is manifested even if there are differences of opinion or character. Love is greater than these differences!

—Angelus, *May 10, 2015*

EVERYDAY HOLINESS

There are people who suffer with a smile and keep the joy of faith despite trials and illnesses. These are the people who carry the Church forward by their everyday holiness, so that they become real beacons in our parishes, our institutions.

When we go to the parishes we meet people who are suffering, who have problems, who have a disabled child or are ill, but they carry on living patiently. These people don't ask for a miracle but live with God's patience, reading the signs of the times. And the world is unworthy of these holy people of God (Hebrews 11). We can also say about these people of ours—people who suffer, suffer so much from so many things but who never lose their smile, keep the joy of faith—that the world isn't worthy of them: it's unworthy! The spirit of the world is unworthy of such people!

"Count it all joy, my brothers, when you meet various trials" (James 1:1–11). What the apostle James says seems rather strange. It almost seems like an invitation to act like a fraud. For how can we enjoy undergoing a trial? "For you know that the testing of your faith produces patience. And let patience have its full effect, that you may be perfect and complete, lacking in nothing."

This is suggesting that we lead our lives according to the rhythm of patience. But patience isn't resignation, it's something else. Actually, patience means carrying life's burdens on our shoulders, things that aren't good, horrible things, things we don't want. That patience is what will help us grow to maturity. Someone without patience wants everything at once, everything in a hurry. And someone who doesn't have the wisdom of patience is a willful person, who ends up acting like a willful child who says, "I want this, I want that, I don't like this," and is never happy with anything.

"Why does this generation ask for a sign?" asks the Lord in the gospel passage from Mark (8:11–13), in reply to a request from the Pharisees. What he meant was that this generation is like children who hear happy music but won't dance and sad music but won't cry. Nothing is right for them! Indeed, someone without patience is someone who doesn't grow, who remains a willful child, who can't take life as it comes and can only say: "Either that or nothing!"

Where there is no patience, one of the temptations is to become willful like children. Another temptation of those who lack patience is wanting to be omnipotent. They demand: "I want this now!" That's what the Lord is referring to when the Pharisees ask him for a sign from heaven. For really, what did they want? They wanted a spectacle, a miracle. Actually, it's the same temptation as the one the devil proposed to Jesus in the wilderness when he urged him to do something—turn these stones into bread and everyone will believe in you, or throw yourself down from the temple to show your power.

But, in asking Jesus for a sign, the Pharisees confuse God's way of working with that of a sorcerer. God has his own way of doing things: God's patience. And every time we go to the sacrament of reconciliation, we sing a hymn to God's patience. The Lord carries us on his back, so patiently!

Christian life must dance to that music of patience, because it was the music of our fathers, the people of God who followed the commandment the Lord gave to our father Abraham: Walk on and be blameless!

The people have suffered so much: they've been persecuted and killed, they have had to hide in caves and caverns. And they were glad, joyful—as the apostle James says—to greet the promises from afar. That's the patience we must have during trials. It's the patience of a grown-up person, God's patience who bears with us, carries us on his back, it's the patience of our people. How patient our people are even now!

There are so many suffering people who carry on their lives with patience. They don't ask for a sign, like the Pharisees, but they know how to read the signs of the times. So they know that when the fig tree sprouts spring is coming. The impatient people described in the gospel wanted a sign, but they didn't know how to read the signs of the times. That's why they didn't recognize Jesus.

The letter to the Hebrews says clearly that the world was unworthy of the people of God. But today we can say the same about those among our people: those who suffer, suffer so much, from so many things but never lose their smile, keep the joy of faith. Yes, the world isn't worthy of them either! It's these people, our people, in our parishes, in our institutions, who carry the Church forward by their everyday holiness, every day.

—*Morning homily, February 17, 2014*

In Weakness We Become Strong

The way we experience illness and disability is an indication of the love we are ready to offer. The way we face suffering and limitation is the measure of our freedom to give meaning to life's experiences, even when they strike us as meaningless and unmerited. Let us not be disturbed, then, by these tribulations (cf. 1 Th 3:3). We know that in weakness we can become strong (cf. 2 Cor 12:10) and receive the grace to fill up what is lacking in the sufferings of Christ for his body, the Church (cf. Col 1:24). For that body, in the image of the risen Lord's own, keeps its wounds, the mark of a hard struggle, but they are wounds transfigured forever by love.

—*Homily, Jubilee for the Sick and Persons with Disabilities, June 12, 2016*

Praying to God for the Living and the Dead

Centrality of Mercy

I am thinking of the prayer groups that Saint Pio called "nurseries of the faith, the fertile soil of love."They were not just centers for happy gatherings with friends and to find support, but *the fertile soil of divine love*. This is what prayer groups are! Prayer, in fact, is a true and proper *mission*, which brings the fire of love to the whole of humanity. Padre Pio used to say that prayer is a "force that moves the world." Prayer is a force that moves the world! Do we believe this? It's true. Try it! He said that it "spreads the smile and the blessing of God over every languor and weakness" (Second International Congress of Prayer Groups, May 5, 1966).

Prayer, then, is not a nice practice for finding a little peace of heart, nor is it a means of devotion for obtaining useful things from God. Were it so, then it would be an act of subtle selfishness: I pray in order to be well, just as if I were taking an aspirin. But this is just making a deal.

No, it's not like this. Prayer is something else, it is something else. Prayer is instead *a spiritual work of mercy*, which

169

means bringing everything to the heart of God. "You take it, you who are Father." It should be like this, speaking to him in a simple way. Prayer is saying: "You, take it, you who are Father. Look at us, you who are Father." This is the relationship with the Father. Prayer is like this. It is a gift of faith and love, an intercession needed just as bread is. In a word, it means *to entrust*: entrust the Church, entrust people, entrust situations to the Father—"I entrust this to you"—so that you will take care of it.

That is why prayer, as Padre Pio liked to say, is "the greatest weapon we have, a key that opens the heart of God." A key that opens God's heart: it is a simple key. The heart of God is not "heavily guarded" with many security measures. You can open it with a common key, with prayer. For his is a heart of love, a father's heart. And it is the Church's greatest strength, one which we must never let go of, for the Church bears fruit only if she does as did Our Lady and the apostles, who "with one accord devoted themselves to prayer" (Acts 1:14) as they awaited the Holy Spirit. Dedicated and united in prayer. Otherwise we risk relying elsewhere for support: on means, on money, on power. Then evangelization vanishes and joy is extinguished and the heart grows dull.

Do you want to have a dull heart? [*The people respond*: No!] Do you want to have a joyful heart? [Yes!] Pray! This is the recipe.

While I thank you for your commitment, I encourage you. May the prayer groups be "centers of mercy": centers that are always open and active, centers through which the humble power of prayer may bring the light of God to the world and the energy of love to the Church.

Padre Pio, who called himself "a poor brother who prays," wrote that prayer is "the highest apostolate that a soul can exercise in the Church of God" (*Epistolario* II, 70). May you always be joyful apostles of prayer! Prayer works miracles. The apostolate of prayer works miracles.

—Address to the Jubilee for Prayer Groups of Padre Pio,
Saint Peter's Square, February 6, 2015

PERSECUTION

Brotherly love is the best testimony we can give that Jesus is alive with us, that Jesus is risen.

Let us pray in a special way for Christians who are suffering persecution. In our day there are so many Christians who are suffering persecution—so, so many, in a great many countries. Let us pray for them, with love, from our heart. May they feel the living and comforting presence of the Risen Lord.

—Regina Coeli, April 14, 2013

THANKS!

Dear friends, I thank you once more for all you have done during these days. Thank you! Do not forget what you have experienced here! You can always count on my prayers, and I know I can count on yours. One last thing: pray for me.

—Meeting with volunteers at the XXVIII World Youth Day,
Rio de Janeiro, July 28, 2013

NEVER WAR!

Tomorrow is the hundredth anniversary of the start of World War I, which had millions of victims and caused immense devastation. This conflict, which Pope Benedict XVI called a "senseless slaughter," led after four long years to a most fragile peace. Tomorrow will be a day of mourning in memory of this tragedy. While remembering this tragic event, I hope that the mistakes of the past are not repeated, that the lessons of history are acknowledged, and that the cause for peace may always prevail through patient and courageous dialogue...Let us remember everything is lost with war and nothing is lost with peace.

Brothers and sisters, never war! Never war! I think mostly of the children, of those who are deprived of the hope for a dignified life, of a future: dead children, wounded children, maimed children, orphaned children, children who have the remnants of war as toys, children who do not know how to smile. Stop, please! I ask you with all my heart. It is time to stop! Stop, please!

—Angelus, *July 27, 2014*

THE UNION BETWEEN HEAVEN AND EARTH

This wonderful communion, this wondrous union between heaven and earth takes place in the highest and most intense way in the liturgy, and especially in the celebration of the Eucharist, which expresses and fulfills the most profound union between the members of the Church. In the

Eucharist, we in fact encounter the living Jesus and his strength, and through him we enter into communion with our brothers and sisters in the faith: those who live with us here on earth and those who have gone before us into the next life, the unending life.

This reality fills us with joy. It is beautiful to have so many brothers and sisters in the faith who walk beside us, supporting us with their help as together we travel the same road toward heaven. And it is comforting to know that there are other brothers and sisters who have already reached heaven, who await us and pray for us, so that together in eternity we can contemplate the glorious and merciful face of the Father.

—Angelus, *Solemnity of All Saints, November 1, 2014*

FAITHFUL DEPARTED

Yesterday we celebrated the solemnity of All Saints, and today the liturgy invites us to commemorate the faithful departed. These two celebrations are intimately linked to each other, just as joy and tears find a synthesis in Jesus Christ, who is the foundation of our faith and our hope. On the one hand, in fact, the Church, a pilgrim in history, rejoices through the intercession of the saints and the blessed who support her in the mission of proclaiming the Gospel; on the other, she, like Jesus, shares the tears of those who suffer separation from loved ones, and like him and through him echoes the thanksgiving to the Father who has delivered us from the dominion of sin and death.

—Angelus, *Solemnity of All Souls, November 2, 2014*

A Culture of Encounter

Let us pray that, with the help of the Lord and the cooperation of all men and women of good will, there will spread ever further a culture of encounter, capable of bringing down all the walls that still divide the world, so that no longer will innocent people be persecuted and even killed on account of their belief and their religion. Where there is a wall, there is a closed heart. We need bridges, not walls!

—Angelus, *November 9, 2014*

Consistency

Today, brothers and sisters, let us pray in a special way for those who are discriminated against, persecuted, and killed for bearing witness to Christ. I would like to say to each one of them: if you bear this cross with love, you have entered into the mystery of Christmas, you are in the heart of Christ and of the Church.

Further, let us pray that, thanks to the sacrifice of the martyrs of today—there are so many, so very many!—the commitment to recognize and concretely ensure religious freedom may be strengthened, as this freedom is an inalienable right of every human being...

And do not forget Christian consistency, which is thinking, feeling, and living as a Christian, not to thinking like a Christian and living as a pagan—not this! Today let us ask St. Stephen for the grace of Christian consistency. And please continue to pray for me, do not forget!

—Angelus, *Feast of Saint Stephen, Protomartyr, December 26, 2014*

MATERNAL PROTECTION

Let us pause here for a moment and pray in silence for all families in difficulty, whether due to problems of illness, unemployment, discrimination, the need to emigrate, difficulty in understanding each other and lack of union. Let us pray in silence for all these families . . .

Let us entrust to Mary, queen and mother of the family, all the families of the world, that they may live in faith, in accord, in reciprocal aid, and for this I invoke upon them the maternal protection of the One who was the mother and daughter of her Son.

—Angelus, *Feast of the Holy Family, December 28, 2014*

REST IN PRAYER

Dear friends in Christ, know that I pray for you always! I pray for families! I do! I pray that the Lord may continue to deepen your love for him, and that this love may manifest itself in your love for one another and for the Church. Do not forget Jesus who sleeps! Do not forget Saint Joseph who sleeps! Jesus slept with the protection of Joseph. Do not forget: families find their rest in prayer. Do not forget to pray for families. Pray often and take the fruits of your prayer into the world, that all may know Jesus Christ and his merciful love. Please pray also for me, for I truly need your prayers and will depend on them always! Thank you very much!

—Meeting with families, *Manila, January 16, 2015*

A Prayer for Cristal

Yesterday, as Mass was about to begin, one of the towers fell, like that one over there, and injured a young lady working there and she died. Her name is Cristal. She was helping in the organization of that Mass. She was twenty-seven years old. She was young like you and she was working for a group called "Catholic Relief Services." She was a volunteer.

I would like all of us, together, you who are young people just like her, to stop for a moment of silence to pray, and then to call upon our heavenly Mother. Let us pray. (Silence . . . Ave Maria)

Let us also say a prayer for her mother and father. She was their only child. Her mother is flying in from Hong Kong. Her father has come to Manila to wait for her mother. (Our Father)

—*Meeting with youth, Manila, January 18, 2015*

Renewed Commitment

Dear brothers and sisters, today is the World Leprosy Day. I express my closeness to all the people who suffer from this contagion, as well as to those who care for them, and to those who struggle to remove the causes of the disease, that is to say, living conditions unworthy of man. Let us renew our commitment of solidarity to these brothers and sisters!

—Angelus, *January 25, 2015*

THE SCANDAL OF WAR

Once again my thoughts go to the beloved people of Ukraine. Unfortunately the situation is deteriorating and the polarity between the parties is growing worse.

Let us pray first and foremost for the victims, among whom are so many civilians, and for their families, and let us ask the Lord that this horrible fratricidal violence may cease as quickly as possible. I renew this heartfelt appeal in order that every effort—on the international level as well—may be made for the reopening of dialogue, the only possible way to restore peace and harmony in that tortured land.

Brothers and sisters, when I hear the words "victory" or "defeat" I feel great sorrow, great sadness in my heart. They are not just words; the only just word is "peace." This is the only just word. I am thinking of you, Ukrainian brothers and sisters . . . Think, this is a war among Christians! You all share one baptism! You are fighting with Christians. Think about this scandal. And let us all pray, for prayer is our protest before God in times of war.

—*General Audience, Saint Peter's Square, February 4, 2015*

HEALTH OF THE SICK

Let us pray to Mary, Health of the Sick, that every person who is sick might experience, thanks to the care of those who are close to them, the power of God's love and the comfort of her maternal tenderness.

—*Angelus, February 8, 2015*

A DISGRACEFUL SCOURGE

Dear brothers and sisters, today, February 8, is the feast of Saint Josephine Bakhita, a Sudanese nun who as a child had the traumatic experience of being a victim of human trafficking. The Unions of Superiors and Superiors General of Religious Institutes have organized a *Day of Prayer and Awareness against Human Trafficking*. I encourage those who work helping the men, women, and children who are enslaved, exploited, abused as instruments of work or pleasure, and who are often tortured and mutilated. It is my hope that government leaders may work decisively to remove the causes of this disgraceful scourge, a scourge unworthy of society. May each one of us feel committed to being a voice for our brothers and sisters who have been humiliated and whose dignity has been dishonored. Let us all pray to Our Lady for them and for their family members.

—Angelus, *February 8, 2015*

PRAYER FOR VICTIMS

Dear brothers and sisters, dramatic news of violence, kidnapping, and harassment aimed at Christians and other groups continues to arrive from Syria and Iraq. I want to assure those suffering in such situations that we will not forget them, that we are close to them and are praying that a stop be put to this intolerable violence of which they are victims. Together with members of the Roman Curia last Friday I offered the last Mass of the Spiritual Exercises for this intention. At the same time I ask all, according to their capabilities, to work to alleviate the suffering of those being tried, often only because of the faith they profess. Let us pray for these, our brothers and sisters who are suffering for the faith in Syria and Iraq... Let us pray in silence...

I would also like to call to mind Venezuela, which is again undergoing moments of acute tension. I pray for the victims and, in particular, for the boy killed a few days ago in San Cristóbal. I exhort everyone to reject violence and to respect the dignity of every person and the sacredness of human life, and I encourage them to take up the common path for the good of the country, opening again space for encounter and sincere and constructive dialogue. I entrust that beloved nation to the motherly intercession of Our Lady of Coromoto.

—Angelus, *March 1, 2015*

AN END TO PERSECUTION

Dear brothers and sisters, with sorrow, with much sorrow, I learned of today's terrorist attacks on two churches in the city of Lahore, Pakistan, which caused many deaths and injuries. They are Christian churches. Christians are being persecuted. Our brothers and sisters are spilling their blood solely because they are Christians. While I assure the victims and their families of my prayers, I ask the Lord, I implore the Lord, source of all goodness, for the gift of peace and accord for that country. May there be an end to this persecution of Christians, which the world tries to hide, and may there be peace.

—Angelus, *March 15, 2015*

HUMAN DIGNITY

Dear neighbors, dear brothers and sisters, let us together pray, work, and commit ourselves to ensuring that every family has dignified housing, access to drinking water, a toilet, reliable sources of energy for lighting, cooking, and improving their homes; that every neighborhood has streets, squares, schools, hospitals, areas for sport, recreation and art; that basic services are provided to each of you; that your appeals and your pleas for greater opportunity can be heard; that all can enjoy the peace and security which they rightfully deserve on the basis of their infinite human dignity.

—Visit to the Kangemi slum, Nairobi, Kenya, November 27, 2015

AWAITING THE FINAL AWAKENING

Yesterday and today, many have been visiting cemeteries, which, as the word itself implies, is the "place of rest," as we wait for the final awakening. It is lovely to think that it will be Jesus himself to awaken us. Jesus himself revealed that the death of the body is like a sleep from which he awakens us. With this faith we pause—even spiritually—at the graves of our loved ones, of those who loved us and did us good. But today we are called to remember everyone, even those whom no one remembers. We remember the victims of war and violence; we remember the many "little ones" of the world, crushed by hunger and poverty; we remember the anonymous who rest in paupers' graves. We remember our brothers and sisters killed because they were

Christian; and we remember those who sacrificed their lives to serve others. We especially entrust to the Lord those who have left us during the past year.

Church tradition has always urged prayer for the deceased, in particular by offering the eucharistic celebration for them; it is the best spiritual help that we can give to their souls, particularly to those who are the most forsaken. The foundation of prayer is in the communion of the Mystical Body.

Remembering the dead, caring for their graves, and praying for those who have died are the testimony of confident hope, rooted in the certainty that death does not have the last word on human existence, for human beings are destined to a life without limits, which has its roots and its fulfillment in God.

With this faith in humanity's supreme destiny, we now turn to Our Lady, who suffered the tragedy of Christ's death beneath the cross and took part in the joy of his resurrection. May she, the Gate of Heaven, help us to understand more and more the value of prayer for the souls of the dead. They are close to us! May she support us on our daily pilgrimage on earth and help us to never lose sight of life's ultimate goal, which is Heaven. And may we go forth with this hope that never disappoints!

—Angelus, *Solemnity of All Souls, November 2, 2014*

Victims of Violence

This afternoon I shall go to Verano Cemetery and celebrate Holy Mass there. I will spiritually join those who in these days are visiting cemeteries, the place of rest for those who preceded us with the sign of faith and who wait for the day of resurrection. In particular I will pray for victims of violence, especially for the Christians who have lost their lives because of persecution. I will also pray in a special way for our brothers and sisters—men, women, and children—who have died of thirst or hunger or from exhaustion on the journey to find a better life. In recent days we have seen those terrible desert images in the newspapers. Let us all pray in silence for these brothers and sisters of ours.

—Angelus, *Solemnity of All Saints, November 1, 2013*

COMMUNION

Praying for the dead is, first and foremost, a sign of appreciation for the witness they have left us and the good that they have done. It is giving thanks to the Lord for having given them to us and for their love and their friendship. The Church prays for the deceased in a particular way during Holy Mass. The priest states: "Be mindful, O Lord, of thy servants who are gone before us with the sign of faith, and rest in sleep of peace. To these, O Lord, and to all that sleep in Christ, grant we beseech thee a place of refreshment, light and peace" (Roman Canon). It is a simple, effective, meaningful remembrance, because it entrusts our loved ones to God's mercy. We pray with Christian hope that they may be with him in Paradise, as we wait to be together again in that mystery of love which we do not comprehend but which we know to be true because it is a promise that

Jesus made. We will all rise again and we will all be forever with Jesus, with him.

Remembering the faithful departed must not cause us to forget to also *pray for the living*, who together with us face the trials of life each day. The need for this prayer is even more evident if we place it in the light of the profession of faith which states: "I believe in the communion of saints." It is the mystery which expresses the beauty of the mercy that Jesus revealed to us. The communion of saints, indeed, indicates that we are all immersed in God's life and live in his love. All of us, living and dead, are in communion, that is, as a union—united in the community of those who have received baptism and of those who are nourished by the body of Christ and form part of the great family of God. We are all the same family, united. For this reason we pray for each other.

How many different ways there are to pray for our neighbor! They are all valid and accepted by God if done from the heart. I am thinking in a particular way of the mothers and fathers who bless their children in the morning and in the evening. There is still this practice in some families: blessing a child is a prayer. I think of praying for sick people when we go to visit them and pray for them, of silent intercession, at times tearful, in the many difficult situations that require prayer.

Yesterday a good man, an entrepreneur, came to Mass at Santa Marta. That young man will have to close his factory because he cannot manage, and he wept, saying: "I don't want to leave more than fifty families without work. I could declare the company bankrupt: I could go home with my money, but my heart would weep for these fifty families the rest of my life." This is a good Christian who prays through his works: he came to Mass to pray that the Lord might give him a way out, not only for him but for the fifty families. This is a man who knows how to pray, with his heart and through his deeds; he knows how to pray for his neighbor. He is in a difficult situation, and he is not seeking the easiest way out: "Let them manage on their own." This man is a Christian. It did me good to listen to him! Perhaps there are many like him today, at this time in which so many people are in difficulty because of a lack of work. However, I also think of giving thanks for the good news about a friend, a relative, a co-worker: "Thank you Lord, for this wonderful thing!" This too is praying for others, thanking the Lord when things go well.

At times, as Saint Paul says, "we do not know how to pray as we ought, but the Spirit himself intercedes for us with sighs too deep for words" (Rom 8:26). It is the Spirit who prays in us. Therefore, let us open our hearts to enable the Holy Spirit, scrutinizing our deepest aspirations, to purify them and lead them to fulfillment. However, for us and for others, let us always ask that God's will be done, as in the *Our Father*, because his will is surely the greatest good, the goodness of a Father who never abandons us: we must pray and let the Holy Spirit pray in us.

This is beautiful in life: to pray, thanking and praising the Lord, asking for something, weeping when there are difficulties, like that man. But let the heart always be open to the Spirit, that he may pray in us, with us, and for us.

—General Audience, November 30, 2016

IV

CONCLUSION

Blessed Are the Merciful

Jesus Christ is the face of the Father's mercy. These words might well sum up the mystery of the Christian faith. Mercy has become living and visible in Jesus of Nazareth, reaching its culmination in him. The Father, "rich in mercy" (Eph 2:4), after having revealed his name to Moses as "a God merciful and gracious, slow to anger and abounding in steadfast love and faithfulness" (Ex 34:6), has never ceased to show, in various ways throughout history, his divine nature. In the "fullness of time" (Gal 4:4), when everything had been arranged according to his plan of salvation, he sent his only Son into the world, born of the Virgin Mary, to reveal his love for us in a definitive way. Whoever sees Jesus sees the Father (cf. Jn 14:9). Jesus of Nazareth, by his words, his actions, and his entire person reveals the mercy of God.

We need constantly to contemplate the mystery of mercy. It is a wellspring of joy, serenity, and peace. Our salvation depends on it. Mercy: the word reveals the very mystery of the Most Holy Trinity. Mercy: the ultimate and supreme act by which God comes to meet us. Mercy: the fundamental law that dwells in the heart of every person who looks sincerely into the eyes of his brothers and sisters on the path of life. Mercy: the bridge that connects God and man, opening our hearts to the hope of being loved forever despite our sinfulness...

In the parables devoted to mercy, Jesus reveals the nature of God as that of a Father who never gives up until he has forgiven the wrong and overcome rejection with compassion and mercy. We know these parables well, three in particular: the lost sheep, the lost coin, and the father with two sons (cf. Lk 15:1–32). In these parables, God is always presented as full of joy, especially when he pardons. In them we find the core of the Gospel and of our faith, because mercy is presented as a force that overcomes everything, filling the heart with love and bringing consolation through pardon.

In another parable we find an important teaching for our Christian lives. Replying to Peter's question about how many times it is necessary to forgive, Jesus says: "I do not say seven times, but seventy times seven times" (Mt 18:22). He then goes on to tell the parable of the "ruthless servant," who, called by his master to return a huge amount, begs him on his knees for mercy. His master cancels his debt. But when he meets a fellow servant who owes him a few cents and who in turn begs on his knees for mercy, the first servant refuses his request and throws him into jail. When the master hears of the matter, he becomes infuriated and, summoning the first servant again, says to him, "Should not you have had mercy on your fellow servant, as I had mercy on you?" (Mt 18:33). Jesus concludes, "So also my heavenly Father will do to every one of you, if you do not forgive your brother from your heart" (Mt 18:35).

This parable contains a profound teaching for all of us. Jesus affirms that mercy is not only an action of the Father but becomes a criterion for ascertaining who his true children are. In short, we are called to show mercy because mercy has first been shown to us. Pardoning offences becomes the clearest expression of merciful love, and for us Christians it is an imperative from which we cannot excuse ourselves. At times how hard it seems to forgive! And yet pardon is the instrument placed into our fragile hands to attain serenity of heart. To let go of anger, wrath, violence, and revenge are necessary conditions to living joyfully. Let us therefore heed the apostle's exhortation: "Do not let the sun go down on your anger" (Eph 4:26). Above all, let us listen to the words of Jesus who made mercy an ideal of life and a criterion for the credibility of our faith: "Blessed are the merciful, for they shall obtain mercy" (Mt 5:7)—the beatitude to which we should particularly aspire in this Holy Year.

As we can see in sacred scripture, mercy is a key word that indicates God's action toward us. He does not limit himself merely to affirming his love, but makes it visible and tangible. Love, after all, can never be just an abstraction. By its very nature, it indicates something concrete: intentions, attitudes, and behaviors that are shown in daily living. The mercy of God is his loving concern for each one of us. He feels responsible, that is, he desires our wellbeing and he wants to see us happy, full of joy, and peaceful. This is the path which the merciful love of Christians must also travel. As the Father loves, so do his children. Just as he is merciful, so we are called to be merciful to each other...

The Church is commissioned to announce the mercy of God, the beating heart of the Gospel, which in its own way must penetrate the heart and mind of every person. The spouse of Christ must pattern her behavior after the Son of God who went out to everyone without exception. In the present day, as the Church is charged with the task of the new evangelization, the theme of mercy needs to be proposed again and again with new enthusiasm and renewed pastoral action. It is absolutely essential for the Church and for the credibility of her message that she herself live and testify to mercy. Her language and her gestures must transmit mercy, so as to touch the hearts of all people and inspire them once more to find the road that leads to the Father.

May the Church echo the word of God that resounds strong and clear as a message and a sign of pardon, strength, aid, and love. May she never tire of extending mercy, and may she be ever patient in offering compassion and comfort. May the Church become the voice of every man and woman and repeat confidently without end: "Be mindful of your mercy, O Lord, and your steadfast love, for they have been from of old" (Ps 25:6).

—Misericordiae Vultus, *Bull of Induction of the Extraordinary Jubilee of Mercy, April 11, 2015*